DESIGN FOR TEACHING AND TRAINING

A Self-Study Guide
to Lesson Planning

LeRoy Ford

Bud- my friend

LeRoy Ford

BROADMAN PRESS
Nashville, Tennessee

To
Ing. Alfonso Bernal Sahagún
Christian gentleman and educator
Universidad Nacional Autónoma de Mexico
Through an incredible series of events
he made possible for me
a learning experience
rich in all the domains of learning

© Copyright 1978 ● Broadman Press
All rights reserved.
Item code: 4234-22
ISBN: 0-8054-3422-2
Library of Congress catalog card number: 77-87249
Dewey Decimal classification: 268.6
Subject headings: TEACHING // RELIGIOUS EDUCATION
Printed in the United States of America

CONTENTS

If you read this Foreword . . .

you're a lot less likely . . .

. . . to get caught by surprise . . .
AS YOU STUDY THIS BOOK!!

This Foreword answers a lot of questions—like these:

In a Foreword a writer usually tells why he wrote the book. Then he tells about all the people who helped him write it. You may want to skip all of this—but you'll get a lot more out of the course if you find answers to these questions:

1. *Who needs to study this book, anyway?*—Several persons and groups. Maybe you fit into one of these categories:
* Sunday School teachers and other church leaders. Granted, most leaders' guides contain good lesson plans. But every teacher and trainer ought to have the experience of designing a lesson plan.
* *Persons who write study materials for use in Theological Education by Extension,* or TEE as they call it on the mission fields. The format of the book may serve as one model for designing a course. Besides that, it will provide enough learning theory to help them prepare study books which help people learn.
* *Public school teachers and professors in colleges and universities.*— The approach used in this book pulls together the three parts of a lesson plan: goals and indicators (objectives), learning activities, and tests. Most teachers have to make lesson plans—and many have to do them in terms of learner competencies. You've come to the right place.
* *Editors who produce lesson course materials for schools and churches.*—Editors have to judge the worth of lesson plans. This book will help them do it.
* *Writers of teaching and training procedures for periodicals.*— Writers need to know their subject well. But they also need enough understanding of how persons learn to make the procedures worth the using.
* *Anybody who **wants** to do original lesson planning—or who **must do** original lesson planning.* That means anybody who doesn't want to depend all the time on plans someone else designed.

2. *How does this book differ from the usual one?* First of all, it *does* differ from most other books.
* *The self-study format allows you to study it by yourself* and receive many of the benefits you would get with a private teacher or trainer. The book contains dozens of "practice cycles" which help you learn and help you know how well you have learned. A practice cycle has three parts: (1) An "imput" paragraph which presents a

concept in much the same way any other book presents ideas. You can read that part all the way through just as you would read a book. (2) A practice item that lets you prove to yourself that you understand the "input." These items ask you to respond actively by either discrimination among possible answers to problems or composing an answer. (3) Feedback which tells you what most people would call the right answer. It explains why one answer fits and another doesn't. Of course, you can have your own opinion!

You can study at your own pace. You'll find an activity at the end of each unit where you can prove to yourself how much you have learned. You will want to purchase the *Leader's Guide* for this book. It contains two *mastery tests* for each unit in this book. You may use them as pretests or as posttests.

Each unit has a page at the beginning which tells you what you may expect to learn from studying the unit. It states the learning goal and the "indicators" which prove you have learned.

You will find a note at the beginning of each unit which tells you the approximate time you will need to complete the unit.

* *Dozens of people have "validated" the material before you got it in this book form*. That means many people have studied the material and taken tests over it. Then the writer rewrote the book in the light of what they did or did not learn. Testing (validation) continued until 90 percent of the people in the target group did each activity and test item correctly. Each person took "delayed posttests" about ten days after studying each unit. Those tests became the basis for change in the course. So, you should not only learn from the material but you should retain it longer than if you had studied some other way.

Sixty adults in eight churches studied the material. They took a total of about eighteen hundred tests over the material. First they took a pretest over each unit to discover what they already knew and understood. Then they took the tests at the end of each unit. Then a day or two after they completed the unit they took another test. Then ten days later came the "delayed posttest" which served as a basis for revision of the material. The churches included University Baptist Church, Fort Worth; Gambrell Street Baptist Church, Fort Worth; Birchman Avenue Baptist Church, Fort Worth; Western Hills Baptist Church, Fort Worth; Geyer Springs Baptist Church, Little Rock; and Reece Prairie Baptist Church, near Fort Worth.

Thirty-five students at Southwestern Baptist Theological Seminary, Fort Worth, studied the material during one semester. They took over a thousand tests which provided data for revising the course.

In both the seminary and in the churches, group members studied only the material. They did not receive any other instruction in groups or otherwise. So the validation reflects what the target group learned from study of the book only.

Validation has progressed enough for us to make these predictions:

(1) Ninety percent of the target group members will respond correctly to each activity and test item.

(2) About 85 percent will show ability to write goals, indicators, activities, and tests of their own, using new material as a basis.

(3) About 85 percent or more will show ability to watch a videotaped teaching model and reconstruct the lesson plan used in the model.

(4) About 75 percent will show ability to write a lesson plan according to the plan the book presents, and can teach or lead the session.

The book differs in another way. It constitutes only one part of a collection of materials designed to help learners reach learning goals. These materials include (1) this book which presents the three aspects of the lesson planning process; and (2) a *Leader's Guide* which contains tests, audiotapes, and transparencies for the overhead projector. Hopefully, four videotaped teaching models will be available at a later date. Trainees will analyze the tapes and reconstruct the lesson plans the teacher uses.

All of these parts, put together and interrelated, make up what we call an "instructional system."

3. *In what ways may one use this book?* Well, in at least three ways.

* Use it as a self-study guide. Study it without any outside help from a leader. The writer designed the book for just this kind of use. Use the mastery tests in *Leader's Guide* to test your progress. You may also consider the last activity in each unit as a test.

* *Use it for "homework" before meeting with a training group.* If your church or school decides to conduct training workshops in lesson planning, the leader will use the *Leader's Guide* and the other aids in planning the sessions.

* *Use all or part of the book.* These approaches will help you decide how to use the book:

Select units at random. Each unit in a real sense stands alone. For example, if you want to study how to teach and train for understanding, choose unit 7, and so on. Do all the activities. *Take a short cut through the book by selecting a sequence of units.* For example, units 1, 3, 6, 7, 8, 10, 12, and 13 make a good combination of related units. Do all the activities in those units. *Use all the book.* If you study all the book you should have a good grasp of the many aspects of lesson planning used in education today. Do all the activities in all the units.

Take the accelerated route throughout the book. You may want to read the book like you read any other book. If so, read the material in *light* type in each unit. Of course you will miss those aspects of the course which cause learning to endure.

4. *Who fits into the target group for this material?* Those who helped test the material before it came to you had a high school education or above. Most had one or more years of college. However, some did well who had less than a high school education. Those who prefer much simpler courses may study *Primer for Teachers and Leaders* by LeRoy Ford. Those who prefer more depth may study the *Primer* also, but they should study this book. Those who tested the material included Sunday School teachers and other church leaders, all adults; public-school teachers and persons preparing for Christian ministry. You can probably do well in a study of this book but you will have to work hard. But then we know pretty well that if you consider yourself in this target group you will do well.

5. *Will the book do all things for all teachers and trainers?* No. Neither will a lot of other things! It deals primarily with lesson planning. Study this material and you will learn to write lesson plans. The book does not deal with all that a leader needs to learn to do well. But it deals with a very important part of it.

The book does not deal directly with the developmental aspects of learning. That remains for another book. Teachers and trainers can, however, study the principles and adapt them in the light of what they know and understand about age level abilities and concepts. In short, each learner differs from all the others. He differs in age, appearance, likes and dislikes, background, experience, talents, and ability to learn. In other pictures . . .

Your pupil is himself!

This————————————

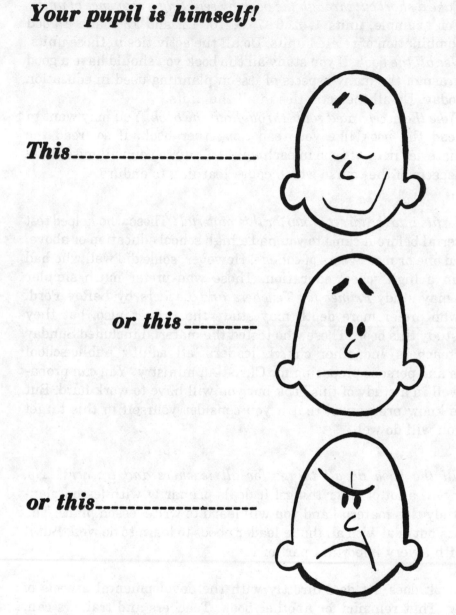

or this—————

or this——————————

may be your pupil.

He differs from all the others. Treat him accordingly!

And because you understand the value of flipcharts and have all skill in using them, you won't get into situations like this! Or will you?

Mrs. Wade (Judy) Stamey did more than any other person in guiding this instructional system through the validation process. She supervised validation of the material in a class in principles of teaching at Southwestern Baptist Theological Seminary. Then she, along with other graduate seminar students in religious education, validated the material in seven churches in the Fort Worth, Texas, area. Mrs. Stamey scored hundreds upon hundreds of tests, drew inferences from the data, and provided suggestions for revision.

She has tried the system with training groups—and it works!

All cartoons except those otherwise identified, are based on the author's original stick-figure drawings. Interpretations of the originals have been made by Doug Dillard, Joe McCormick, and Doug Jones.

GOALS
AND
INDICATORS

UNIT 1

Hitch Your Teaching and Training to a Goal!

Why You Will Find the Study Useful:

The learning goals you will learn to write
will help you prepare good lesson plans.
Learning goals give you all sorts of
clues as to the kinds of activities to use.

What You May Expect to Learn:

Goal: A study of this unit should help you
understand the process of writing learning
goals.

**Some Things You Will Do to Prove You Have Achieved the Goal
for This Study:**

>   *Indicators:*
>
>   * Write learning goals for use in lesson plans.
>   * Recognize a good goal statement when you see one.
>   * Select from a list of definitions the one which
>   best defines "goal."
>   * Define "diffusion of learning" (overlapping of
>   learning outcomes).
>   * List and explain the four primary learning
>   outcomes (kinds of learning).
>   * Identify the parts of stated learning goals.
>   * List the four characteristics of a learning goal.

You will need about 55 minutes to complete this unit.

Preview of Terms Used in This Unit:

Goal.—A somewhat broad statement of what a pupil needs to learn. It tells the kind of learning and states the subject in a "chewable bite."

Primary learning outcome.—The *kind* of learning the pupil should acquire—knowledge, understanding, skill, attitudes, and values.

Learning.—Learning means a lasting change in knowledge, understanding, skill, attitudes, and values, brought about by experience.

Knowledge.—In this unit, knowledge means facts and information.

Understanding.—In this unit, understanding means comprehension of how facts and ideas relate one to another, and ability to put knowledge to practical use.

Skill.—In this unit, skill (psychomotor skill) means the ability to perform with ease a physical act.

Attitudes.—In this unit, attitudes means a point of view toward a person, place, thing, or idea.

Diffusion of Learning.—This term sounds complicated but it simply means the "overlapping" that occurs when one studies for one particular kind of learning. For example, when one gains understanding, he also develops some change in attitude and knowledge as a result.

15

UNIT 1

Hitch Your Teaching and Training to a Goal!

Thomas Edison said, "There must be a better way! Find it!" He had the right idea. There must be a better way to plan lessons. Let's find it. Sooner or later most teachers and leaders have to plan their own lessons. They have to throw away their crutches! They may not like the lesson plans in the *Leader's Guide*. So they decide to do their own. They may not even have a *Leader's Guide*! So they go to the drawing board. They do their own teaching and training plans. Then some leaders just prefer to do their own thing! If you come within one of these groups— and want to do better lesson planning—then you'll find help in this course.

The course deals with the three basic parts of a lesson plan. These include goals, learning activities (methods), and ways to determine whether anybody learned anything. In this course you will learn to write goals. You will learn how to plan methods and activities to help the pupil reach the goals. Then you will learn how to "test" to find out whether the pupil has learned. (If you want a sneak preview of what a lesson plan looks like, look at the very simple lesson plans in Unit 13.)

Units 1 and 2 will help you learn to write goals and "indicators." (Don't worry about the term "indicator" right now.) Unit 3 presents the lesson planning process. Units 4 through 11 will help you learn to plan the right kinds of learning activities. Unit 12 will teach you to "test" whether pupils have learned. Unit 13 will help you "put it all together." You will see how goals, activities, and tests fit together to make a lesson plan.

You probably have not read a book like this one before. In fact, you cannot "read it like a book."

After each main idea you will find a learning activity. It asks you to respond in some way to the idea. Many books include activities or questions at the end of each chapter. But persons learn better when activities or questions appear *immediately after* a new idea appears. Following the activity, you will find a "feedback" statement. It explains why certain answers in the activity are right or wrong and why.

In short, the book acts like a teacher. It asks what a teacher or leader would ask if the leader were with you! If you can accept this "different" style, you will make better progress. This book will help you master the lesson planning process—at your own pace. You'll need to look elsewhere for leisure reading!

At the beginning of each unit you will find a set of goals and "indicators." They outline what you should learn to do because you have studied the chapter. You may have not seen this in a book before. Read the goals before you start work on a unit.

Now, let's learn to write learning goals. Read again, *now,* the goals and "indicators" which precede this unit.

Planning makes things happen which would not otherwise occur. Builders start with plans—blueprints. Teachers start with lesson plans. Good lesson plans begin with goals. [1] However, not all teachers begin with goals! They teach—then race to move the target to where the arrow went!

The goal-hitching teacher understands the process of writing learning goals. The preceding sentence contains the goal for this chapter. It's not exactly a needle in a haystack, so *read again the first sentence in this paragraph.* Underline the phrase which describes what you should learn as a result of studying this unit. As a result of study of this chapter, the teacher (the learner in this case) "understands the process of writing learning goals."

One may learn the process of writing a learning goal by observing four characteristics of a well-stated goal.

To see in advance what a learning goal looks like, read the following examples. Then later you will have an opportunity to determine what they contain and how to write them.

1. The pupil understands the effects of smoking on health.
2. The pupil knows the Beatitudes.
3. The pupil demonstrates an attitude of concern for the physical needs of retarded children.
4. The pupil demonstrates skill in playing the trumpet.

Note that some of the statements say the pupil *demonstrates* a kind of learning. Others simply say he *understands* or *knows*. Either style serves the purpose.

Each of these learning goals has four characteristics. Let's look at the first one.

---

[1] This unit deals only with goals. Unit 2 deals with the more specific objectives or indicators which tell what a learner does to prove he has learned.

● 1. *A goal tells in relatively broad terms what the pupil should learn.*— Instead of stating what the learner will *do to prove* he has learned, it sets in relatively broad terms the direction of learning.

■ **To acquire some understanding of the concept of "broadness," read the following statements. Check those which you consider "relatively broad" statements of learning intent.**

_____ 1. **The student arranges in chronological order a random list of ten events in the life of Jesus.**

_____ 2. **The student knows the teachings of Jesus.**

_____ 3. **The student matches ten theological terms with a list of definitions.**

_____ 4. **The student demonstrates understanding of the meanings of theological terms.**

_____ 5. **The student understands the lesson planning process.**

The list contains some very specific statements—one and three. They specify rather minute indicators that the learner has achieved a goal. So we do not call them goals. (Unit 2 will deal with these specific statements, so we will not consider them now.) Numbers two, four, and five express learning intent in relatively board terms.

■ **We can "picture" the concepts of "broadness" and "specificness" visually. Which of the following drawings pictures a goal?**

_____ 1. [ ]

_____ 2. [ ]

Of course you checked number one.

19

Some writers call the relatively broad statements by other names. Some call them "general instructional objectives." [2] Others simply call them "objectives." A goal by any other name would sound as broad and general. Along with most other writers, we prefer to call them goals.

[2] Norman E. Gronlund, *Stating Behavioral Objectives for Classroom Use,* London: The Macmillan Company, 1970, p. 4.

● 2. *Goals tell what should happen to the learner, not the teacher!*—Goals do not express what the *teacher* will know or understand. They do not state what the teacher will do to teach the lesson or the course. They tell what happens or will happen to the learner. For example, the following statement tells what will have happened to the learner at the end of a course.

Knows the Rules of Grammar

■ **Which of these goals describes what will happen to the learner rather than what the teacher will do to teach?**

_____ 1. **Understands the methods of Bible study.**

_____ 2. **To increase the student's understanding of the methods of Bible study.**

In number 1, the student obviously understands the methods of Bible study. Number 2 tells what the teacher intends to do. You should have checked number one.

■ **Write the first two characteristics of a goal:**

1. _____

2. _____

You should have written: 1. "relatively broad statement of what the learner should learn. 2. "tells what should happen to the learner—not the teacher."

3. *Goals indicate the kind of learning or change which the learner should achieve.*—A discussion of this characteristic requires more space than that used for the first one. (We just wanted to let you know.)

Different kinds of change may take place in the learner. Learners change in what they *know*. That means they can recall facts and information. Their *attitudes* change. That means they change in the way they feel about persons, places and things. They change in ability to perform motor *skills*. This means they change in what they can do physically. They may also change in *understanding* or in what they comprehend. Students also change in appreciation, creativity, and so on. We call these kinds of change *"primary learning outcomes."* This book treats four of them: (1) knowledge, (2) understanding, (3) attitudes, and (4) skills.

Usually the goal expresses the primary learning outcome in just one word. It tells whether the learner will understand something, know something, acquire an attitude about something, or develop skill in doing something.

■ *In the following statement, underline the* one word *which indicates the primary learning outcome:*

The learner demonstrates skill in locating Bible references.

The statement says nothing about attitudes, understanding, or knowledge. (As we shall learn later it involves these outcomes to some extent.) It states skill. The learner finds Bible references by physically handling the Bible. True, he must know certain things—like the names of books of the Bible. But this goal deals primarily with skill.

22

● In stating learning goals, the teacher makes a decision as to which learning outcome (kind of learning) will receive primary emphasis. It may relate to a unit of study, a lesson, or a course. The teacher studies pupil needs, the subject matter, and other factors. He then tries to decide wisely which primary learning outcome to use.

When one decides to take a trip, he asks: Does my "goal" require that I travel primarily north, south, east, or west? If he decides to travel primarily north, he admits that at times he may travel east, west, or even south! But in the end he arrives at a place north of the starting point. His decision as to direction determines the states and cities through which he will travel. It helps him know the kinds of clothes to wear, and the methods of travel to use. In the same way, when a teacher selects a primary learning outcome, that decision affects his choice of methods. It affects his choice of activities, learning aids, and resources for use in the lesson or unit of study.

■ *In the following statements, underline the one word which states the primary learning outcome:*

1. *The pupil demonstrates knowledge of the history of Judah.*

2. *The pupil develops an attitude of concern for the emotional needs of blind children.*

3. *The pupil understands the symbolism of the tabernacle.*

4. *The pupil demonstrates skill in beating time in music.*

5. *The pupil demonstrates knowledge of Paul's writings.*

You should have underlined the words knowledge, attitude, understands, skill, and knowledge, in that order. These words indicate the kind of learning expected.

A learning goal, remember, indicates the primary learning outcome (knowledge, understanding, skill, or attitude).

Now, let's find out why we use the word primary.

● In the drawing which follows, the small circle stands for a lesson on "Love Thy Neighbor." The large circle stands for all the kinds of learning. Study the drawing.

■ *Check the statement or statements which tell what the drawing actually says about the lesson. Remember, the small circle stands for the lesson.*

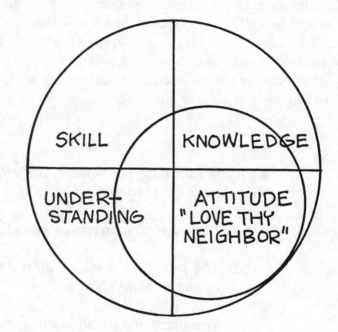

The drawing says:

_____ 1. **One would find it difficult to teach toward one primary outcome without producing as by-products some degree of learning or change in the other outcomes.**

_____ 2. **When one teaches for change in attitude, the pupil will gain some degree of understanding, knowledge, and skill at the same time.**

The drawing says both of the things listed. You should have checked both. A teacher cannot teach for learning in one area only—even if he tries!

24

● A learner who seeks to understand something, also gains some degree of knowledge. And he develops some degree of attitude change. When someone gains knowledge about something, it helps him also to understand. And the knowledge may even change his attitude about the thing. When this happens, we say that *diffusion of learning* has taken place.

■ **Read this case study.**

A pupil developed an understanding of what Methodists believe. In the process, he learned some facts about Methodists. His attitude also changed.

What do we say has taken place? _____

You should have written, "diffusion (or overlapping) of learning." When we say primary learning outcome it means we have decided which of the four outcomes we will stress. But at the same time we accept the fact that other kinds of learning will take place.

● Sometimes the topic or title of a lesson suggests the primary outcome. For example, a topic which deals with facts would call for knowledge as the primary learning outcome. Some subjects deal with explanations and solving of problems. They would call for understanding as the primary learning outcome. The teacher may also study the needs of the pupils to determine the primary learning outcome.

■ *In the following list of subjects, write "knowledge" in front of those which you would classify as knowledge subjects. Write "understanding" in front of those which you would classify as understanding.*

1. _____ **Why water boils**

2. _____ **The meaning of salvation**

3. _____ **Events in the early history of America**

4. _____ **States and capital cities of the United States**

You should have answered: 1. understanding; 2. understanding; 3. knowledge; 4. knowledge.

● Some topics deal with feelings and points of view toward persons, places, things, and ideas. They call for attitude as a learning outcome. Some subjects suggest the need for doing things by moving our muscles in some way. We call this a skill (psychomotor) outcome.

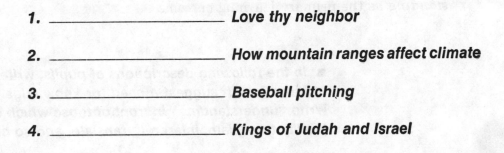

■ *In the blanks in the exercise below, write the appropriate primary outcome involved (knowledge, understanding, attitude, or skill).*

1. _____ *Love thy neighbor*

2. _____ *How mountain ranges affect climate*

3. _____ *Baseball pitching*

4. _____ *Kings of Judah and Israel*

You probably classified the subjects as follows: 1. attitude (deals with point of view toward persons); 2. understanding (explains how); 3. skill (deals with a physical or motor activity); 4. knowledge (deals with facts).

However, teachers could develop any of these topics or themes from more than one viewpoint.

27

● The teacher should study also the pupil and his needs. The needs provide clues as to which learning outcome should receive primary attention. For example, if a pupil cannot explain why Baptists use the congregational form of government, the teacher knows the pupil needs to "understand Baptist polity."

Assume that the pupil could not recall the names of the forms of church government. The teacher would conclude that the learner should gain *knowledge*. If the pupil could not recall facts, the teacher would choose knowledge as the primary learning outcome. If the pupil knew facts but could not explain them, the teacher would choose *understanding* as the primary learning outcome.

■ *In the following descriptions of pupils, write "knowledge" in front of those which suggest a need for knowledge (recall from memory). Write "understanding" in front of those which call for understanding (ability to explain, interpret, translate, and so on).*

1. _____ *The pupil cannot list the names of the books of the Bible.*

2. _____ *The pupil cannot answer satisfactorily questions like, How does "separation of church and state" differ from "a free church in a free state"?*

3. _____ *The pupil cannot recognize a properly stated learning goal when he sees one.*

4. _____ *The pupil cannot locate on a map the states and territories of Mexico.*

You should have answered as follows: (1). knowledge (pupil cannot recall facts and information); (2). understanding (the pupil cannot explain and interpret); (3). understanding (the pupil does not comprehend what constitutes a goal); (4). knowledge (the pupil cannot recall facts and information).

● Some pupils need to change in the way they feel about a person, place, thing, or idea. The teacher then should focus on *attitude* as the primary learning outcome. For example, if a pupil refuses to share toys with other children, the teacher may choose *attitude* change as the primary learning outcome.

If the pupil cannot perform well an act which calls for control of muscles, the teacher would choose *skill* as the kind of learning needed.

■ *Study the following descriptions of pupils. Write which primary learning outcome each calls for (knowledge, understanding, skill, or attitude). Write the outcome in the blanks.*

1. _____ *The pupil dislikes math, especially algebra.*

2. _____ *The pupil cannot type on a typewriter.*

3. _____ *The pupil cannot recite the Ten Commandments.*

4. _____ *The pupil cannot explain what Baptists believe about the Lord's Supper.*

Number 1 suggests attitude *as a needed primary learning outcome. It expresses the pupil's feelings and viewpoint toward math. Number 2 suggests a need for* skill. *It calls for muscular coordination. Number 3 calls for* knowledge. *The learner needs to recall something. Number 4 suggests a need for* understanding. *It requires one to explain and interpret.*

■ *Read the following learning goal. Underline the one word which indicates the primary learning outcome.*

The pupil demonstrates understanding of Robert's Rules of Order.

You should have underlined understanding as the primary learning outcome. This suggests that the learner will do more than simply recall and recite the rules of order. He will accomplish a more difficult kind of learning—understanding.

● At this point, we might define learning goal as follows: "A learning goal is a relatively broad statement of learning intent which expresses from the viewpoint of the learner the primary learning outcome."

■ *You have studied the first three characteristics of a learning goal. Write them below.*

1. _____

2. _____

3. _____

You should have listed these ideas: (1). relatively broad; (2). from viewpoint of learner (what should happen to the learner); and (3). identifies the primary learning outcome.

But goals have at least one other characteristic. Let's learn about it.

● 4. *Goals state the subject dealt with.*—The goal tells the subject with which the lesson or training session will deal. It answers questions like, Understanding of *what*? Knowledge of *what*? Skill in doing *what*? *Which* attitude toward *whom* or *what*?

Learners cannot know everything! They cannot understand everything! The goal needs to tell *what* they will understand, know, do well, and so on. The leader must set up a fence!

As a rule of thumb, the goal limits the subject to a "chewable bite." It limits the subject to what one might study in the time available. For one lesson, it would specify a rather small "bite." For a unit of lessons, it could specify a larger bite.

■ *In the following goal, underline the part which states the subject.*

The learner demonstrates understanding of the causes of the Civil War.

The goal answers the question, Understanding of what? You should have underlined the causes of the Civil War.

● Teachers can apply the "how-long-would-it-take?" test to find out how much of a subject a goal should include. The answers provide clues as to whether to use one session or more than one session in reaching the goal.

The limitation of the subject tells both the teacher and the learner what the lesson or unit *includes* and what it *excludes*. It tells them what to learn and what they don't have to learn. Like a fence, goals include some things; exclude others. The goal should exclude enough of the subject to make it possible to reach the goal in the time available. It should *include* enough to make for worthwhile learning.

■ *Study the following goal statements. Check any which one might deal with in one session. Note that each states a subject but some include too much.*

_____ 1. *The student demonstrates understanding of the Bible.*

_____ 2. *The student demonstrates understanding of Paul's concept of Christian stewardship.*

_____ 3. *The student demonstrates understanding of the four Gospels.*

With some room for argument, number two shows a chewable bite for one session. How long would it take? Probably one session. How long would it take to "understand the Bible"? Eternity! How long would it take to "understand the four Gospels"? A long time! One wants to ask, Understand what about the Bible? Understand what about the four Gospels? The goal specifies the subject. It tells the teacher the content on which to focus.

33

34

■ *Try this simple exercise to clarify how some subjects "include" and "exclude" certain things.*

Study the following list of items. Which one actually includes all the others? Arrange the items, in order, beginning with the one which includes most. Progress to the one which includes the least. (For example, you would assign number "1" to the item which includes all the others.)

_____ *Apples*

_____ *Food*

_____ *Fruit*

All of the items include and exclude something. You probably thought like this: Food includes fruit and fruit includes apples. Fruit excludes all other foods except fruit. It also excludes all things which are not food. Fruit excludes grease pencils and porcupines; antique cars and dollar bills! But fruit also includes many things—kumquats and raspberries; coconuts and watermelons! You probably arranged the items in the order three, one, two.

■ *We can analyze learning goals in the same way. We can arrange than according to the limitation of the subject.*
Which of the following learning goals includes the least amount of the subject?

_____ *1. The pupil understands what Baptists believe.*

_____ *2. The pupil understands what Baptists believe about the church.*

Obviously number two limits the most. If one achieved goal number one he would understand all Baptist doctrines. Number two limits the subject to one doctrine—the doctrine of the church.

GOALS, LIKE BARBED WIRE FENCES, KEEP SOME THINGS IN AND OTHER THINGS OUT!

■ *Study the following learning goals. Arrange them according to limitation of subject. Assign number 1 to the broadest statement; number 3 to the statement which limits the subject most, and so on.*

_____ 1. *The student demonstrates understanding of the effects of drugs on health.*

_____ 2. *The student demonstrates understanding of the effects of heroin on the health of persons ages fifteen to seventeen.*

_____ 3. *The student demonstrates understanding of the effects of heroin on the health of young people.*

You probably arranged them: one, three, two. How long would it take to achieve the goals? The first would require much time. The teacher would have to deal with the effects of all drugs on all people of all age groups. The statement includes all persons regardless of age. The teacher must decide whether the goal limits the subject to a chewable bite. The time needed and the backgrounds of the learners help the leader decide. The second goal tells the leader to deal only with heroin, and only with persons fifteen to seventeen. So number 2 limits the subject most. You would have given it the number "3." Goal number 3 falls in between the others.

■ *In the following goal statement, underline the words which state the subject and limit it.*

The student demonstrates understanding of Paul's concept of justification by faith.

The statement "Paul's concept of justification by faith" states the subject. It answers the question, Understanding of what? It also limits the subject to a "chewable bite."

37

CHECK YOUR PROGRESS

■ *At this point, one of the following statements defines better than the others what learning goal means. One reflects all four characteristics. Check the best definition.*

_____ 1. A learning goal is a relatively broad statement of learning intent which states the primary learning outcome and the subject to be dealt with.

_____ 2. A learning goal is a relatively broad statement of learning intent which states in terms of the student the primary learning outcome and the subject dealt with.

_____ 3. A learning goal is a relatively broad statement of learning intent which states the subject in terms of the student.

Number one omits a reference to "in terms of the student." Number three omits reference to primary learning outcome. Only number two includes all four characteristics.

■ *Now list the four characteristics of a learning goal, without looking at the preceding definitions.*

1. _____

2. _____

3. _____

4. _____

You should have answered with these or similar words: (1). relatively broad statement; (2). from learner's viewpoint; (3). states the primary learning outcome; (4). states the subject in a chewable bite.

■ *Check in the following list of learning goals those which have all four characteristics. Use the four questions shown at the right to help you decide. Ask all four questions each time you analyze a goal.*

Goal Statements	Questions to Ask
_____ 1. **The learner understands terms related to atomic energy.**	**Is the goal relatively broad as opposed to very specific?**
_____ 2. **Instills knowledge of the geography of Palestine.**	**Is the goal stated from the viewpoint of the learner?**
_____ 3. **The learner demonstrates the right attitude.**	**Does the goal state a primary learning outcome?**
_____ 4. **The learner knows the causes of the fall of Rome.**	**Does the goal state the subject? Does it answer one of these questions?**
_____ 5. **The learner lists five of six types of learning aids.**	• **Knowledge of what?** • **Understanding of what?** • **What kind of an attitude and toward whom or what? or** • **Skill in doing what?**

If you asked all four questions in regard to each statement, you checked one and four. Number two expresses the goal from the teacher's viewpoint. It does however, have the other three characteristics. Number 3 does not state which attitude about what nor toward whom. We call number 5 an objective or indicator. You will learn about this kind of statement in the next unit.

■ *Now, for more practice, study the following learning goal statements. Check those which reflect all four characteristics.*

_____ 1. *The student demonstrates an attitude of concern for the financial support of home missions.*

_____ 2. *The student matches the names of states with the state capital cities.*

_____ 3. *To present four events leading to the Babylonian captivity.*

_____ 4. *The student demonstrates understanding of the process of writing learning goals.*

_____ 5. *To discuss the meaning of redemption.*

You should have checked one and four only. Number 2 is too specific and it does not identify a primary learning outcome. Number 3 tells what the teacher, not the pupil, will do. It does not express learning intent from the viewpoint of the learner. Neither does it identify a primary learning outcome. Number 5 omits a primary learning outcome and tells what the teacher will do—not what the pupil will do.

● This chapter has dealt with learning goals. Goals express the essential learnings the student should achieve.

You can do a lot of planning with just the goal.

Learning goals provide clues to the kinds of activities to use. Certain activities tend to work better with one primary learning outcome than with others. For example, certain kinds of learning activities tend to help a person achieve knowledge; others, understanding, and so on. In units 5 through 11 you will learn how to choose the right kinds of activities. Goals also provide clues to teaching resources. They tell you where to look on the resource shelf. Because both teacher and learner know the subject involved, they know which books, learning aids, and other resources to pull off the shelves.

You can do better planning if you can decide how to test to find out whether the pupil has learned. We call these tests "indicators." They "indicate" whether the pupil has reached the learning goal.

Learning goals do not tell how the teacher and the learner will know whether the learner has achieved the goal. That's where unit 2 comes in. The next chapter will provide training in how to write "indicators."

In later chapters you will learn how to use the learning goal and "indicators" to decide on methods and activities.

UNIT 2

Signs of Progress [1]

Why You Will Find the Study Useful:

You can use "indicators" to find out
   whether the pupil has learned. They
   give you clues to learning activities,
   too.

What You May Expect to Learn:

Goal: A study of this unit should help you
   understand the process of writing indicators
   of goal achievement.

**Some Things You Will Do to Prove You Have Achieved the Goal
for This Study:**

   Indicators:

   * Write "indicators" of learning.
   * Recognize a good indicator statement when you see one.
   * Identify the indicator in a goal-indicator statement.
   * Identify the parts of learning indicators.
   * Classify indicators as to type.
   * List the parts of an indicator.

You will need about 45 minutes to complete this unit.

----

[1] *Preparing Instructional Objectives,* Second Edition, Robert F. Mager. Fearon Publishers, Inc., Belmont, California, 1975. Adaptive use of Mager's three characteristics of an objective used by permission of Fearon Publishers, Inc.

Preview of Terms Used in This Unit:

Indicator.—Something the pupil does to prove he has learned. (Many people call them objectives.) You use indicators as a basis for preparing tests. An indicator clearly suggests a test question.

Goal-indicator.—A statement of learning intent which includes both a goal and an indicator.

Action verb.—A word which tells *clearly* a specific action a person does to prove he has learned. (For example: Write, classify, match—as opposed to understand and know.)

Verbal indicators.—An indicator which calls for the pupil to use words orally or in writing.

Discrimination indicator.—An indicator which calls for the pupil to choose between or among things—like matching items in a test.

Motor indicator.—An indicator which calls for the pupil to perform some physical act—like typing or riding a bicycle.

Conditions.—The circumstances under which a pupil will prove he has learned. (For example, this indicator includes a special condition: Given an outline map of Texas, the pupil labels the rivers by name. The leader gives the pupil a map. The pupil does not have to provide it himself.)

UNIT 2

Signs of Progress

In Unit 1 you studied how to write learning goals. Remember, a learning goal sounds something like this:

The learner demonstrates knowledge of the forms of church government.

Note that the statement does four things. (1) It states learning intent in relatively broad terms. (2) It states the intent from the viewpoint of the learner. (3) It specifies the primary learning outcome. (4) It states the subject.

This unit deals with how both teacher and the learner can know when the learner has achieved the goal.

The italicized part of the following statement tells how the learner will prove he has achieved the goal:

The learner demonstrates knowledge of forms of church government *by listing the four major forms.*

We will call the italicized part the "indicator." [1] It *indicates* what the learner will do to indicate (or prove) he has achieved the goal. In this example, the learner lists four forms of church government. This indicates (or proves) that he knows the forms of government.

Everybody looks for indicators or signs of progress. Travelers look for road signs. The signs tell how far one must travel to reach a goal. Even Goldilocks looked for indicators! Temperature indicated the "just rightness" of her soup! Height indicated the "just rightness" of the chairs; softness indicated the "just rightness" of the bed. She kept on testing until she discovered the soup, the chair, and the bed which met her needs.

---

[1] This book uses the term *indicator* instead of "objective." It refers to specific statements of learning intent. "Indicator" reflects in a clearer way the *function* of the statement.

44

Teachers rely on tests as indicators for determining grades. They figure grades on the basis of these indicators or "signs of progress." On tests, learners compose, compute, discriminate, choose, and get red in the face. The teacher observes, then uses what he sees (indicators) to measure progress.

EVERYBODY LOOKS FOR INDICATORS!

● Teachers and leaders need learning goals (relatively broad statements). They also need indicators (statements of what the learner will do to prove he has learned) in order to plan and teach well. "Indicator" means those things the student does to "indicate" he has achieved the learning goal. Indicators tell what the leader will accept as proof that the pupil has moved toward a goal.

Some teachers add the indicators onto the goal statement. Others state the indicators as separate sentences. This unit refers to this combination of goal and indicator as a "goal-indicator."

■ *Read the following goal-indicator. Check the part which tells what the teacher will accept as proof that the pupil has achieved the goal.*

_____ *1. The pupil demonstrates knowledge of . . .*

_____ *2. . . . the location of the mountain ranges of North America . . .*

_____ *3. . . . by writing the names of the mountain ranges in the proper location on an outline map.*

You should have checked three. It states an indicator which the teacher will accept as valid evidence that the learner knows the locations of the mountain ranges. The statement could have called for other kinds of indicators. For this reason, some teachers would say "by doing such things as writing the names of the mountain ranges in the proper locations on a map." This leaves them free to accept other indicators of similar nature. But the teacher in this case decided that this one would provide enough proof.

47

● Before going further in the process of writing indicators, read the following examples. Note that they do not adhere to a prescribed form. But they do contain the essential parts. Reading them will provide in advance a view of what indicators look like. Examples convey the "feel" of indicators in relation to the goals they support. The indicators are in italics.

1. *By doing such things as identifying which of three case studies illustrates the work of a mediator,* the learner demonstrates understanding of what mediator means.

2. The learner demonstrates an attitude of compassion for the emotional needs of retarded children.

   To demonstrate the achievement of this goal, the learner does such things as:

   Volunteers to teach in the special education department at the church.

   Reads a book on emotional needs of children.

   Baby-sits with retarded children.

3. The learner demonstrates knowledge of the geography of Palestine by *doing such things as labeling on an outline map the three primary geographical areas.*

4. The learner understands what learning goal means. To prove achievement of this goal, he does such things as (1) *defines "goal" so as to include the four parts;* (2) *identifies the parts of a given goal.*

Note the varied forms of the four examples. The exact form does not matter as long as each statement includes both the goal and the indicator.

■ *Now, for practice in recognizing indicators, underline the indicators in the following statements.*

1. *The pupil demonstrates understanding of how to give a personal testimony by doing such things as writing his own testimony to include the four parts suggested in the unit.*

2. *By doing such things as matching a list of definitions with a list of ten doctrinal terms, the pupil demonstrates understanding of the meaning of doctrinal terms.*

You should have underlined "by writing his own testimony to include the four elements suggested in the unit" and "by doing such things as matching a list of definitions with a list of ten doctrinal terms."

● In Unit 1 you learned to recognize a properly stated *goal*. How may we recognize a properly stated indicator? Indicators usually have at least three characteristics.

 As a preview, read carefully two or three times, the three characteristics. This unit will then deal with them one at a time.

1. Indicators tell what the learner *does* to indicate or prove he has learned.

2. Indicators tell *how well* the learner should perform.

3. Indicators describe the special *conditions* or circumstances under which the learner will perform.

● Now, let's look at each characteristic separately.

1. *Indicators tell what the learner will do to indicate or prove he has learned.*—Teachers can evaluate only those things they observe pupils doing. This in no way suggests that other learning does not occur. It may occur and does occur, but the teacher does not know that it occurs unless he observes the pupil's actions.

■ **Read the indicator below. Underline the one word which tells what the pupil does to prove he has learned.**

The learner identifies in a list of viewpoints on baptism all those which Baptists hold.

You should have underlined "identifies." The whole indicator includes more than "identifies." But the one word tells what the pupil will do. The verb tells what the pupil will do and what the teacher will observe the pupil doing to indicate learning.

● We express these "doings" in the form of verbs which describe action. The verbs tell precisely what the pupil does. One can almost see him doing the action. The action means the same thing to different people. For example, the word *recite* causes one to picture a person repeating something he has memorized. "Recite" means the same thing to different people. On the other hand, the verb *understand* does not express a specific action. Can a teacher observe a person understanding something? No.

■ *Which of the following indicator statements includes an action verb which a teacher or leader could observe?*

_____ *1. The pupil sees the value of good eating habits.*

_____ *2. The pupil identifies in a case study four violations of good eating habits.*

We would have to classify item one as a "fuzzy." Could a teacher observe a pupil "seeing the value of good eating habits?" No. Number 2 includes an action verb. A teacher could watch as the pupil underlined or in some other way pointed out the four violations of good eating habits. The teacher does not have to watch the pupil answer. He can look at the work the pupil has done and decide whether he has learned.

52

■ *In the following list, check the statements which contain verbs which express an action a teacher could observe.*

_____ 1. Matching two lists of items

_____ 2. Knowing principles of hospital visitation

_____ 3. Understanding theories of inspiration of the Bible

_____ 4. Arranging in chronological order events in Jesus' life

_____ 5. Classifying books of the Bible according to division

_____ 6. Comprehending the meaning of faith

The list contains three statements with action verbs: one, four, five. A teacher could observe a learner "matching," "arranging," and "classifying." He could not observe him "knowing," "understanding," or "comprehending." He needs to ask, How do I know the learner knows, understands, or comprehends?

■ *Read the following indicators. Draw a line under the one verb in each which tells what the learner will do to prove he has learned.*

1. The learner recites the Twenty-third Psalm.

2. The learner identifies the action verbs in given indicators.

3. The learner explains four steps in witnessing to the unsaved.

You should have underlined "recites," "identifies," and "explains." Each describes something a teacher could observe a pupil doing to prove he had achieved goals.

● Indicators come in many forms. Sometimes the verb indicates the learner will write or say something. He may write a word in a blank or write a definition. He may tell a story or recite an assignment. We call these indicators *verbal* indicators. Verbal indicators require the learner to do something with words. We classify indicators as verbal only when the learner *says something* or *writes something out*. He writes, lists, composes, paraphrases, explains, and so on.

■ **Which of the following includes a verbal indicator?**

_____ *1. The learner writes a translation of John 3:15 from the original Greek.*

_____ *2. The learner classifies a given sermon as to type.*

Number 1 says the learner "writes." He composes—puts words on paper. We call it a verbal indicator. In number 2 the pupil neither writes nor speaks. He classifies.

54

■ *Now, check in this longer list the verbal indicators. Remember, the pupil may use either oral or written responses.*

_____ 1. *The learner counsels a parent of a drug addict. (Ask, Does the learner say or write something in order to "counsel"?)*

_____ 2. *The learner assembles a Model XYZ projector. (Does the learner need to say or write something in order to "assemble"?)*

_____ 3. *The learner writes a paper on how to saddle a horse.*

_____ 4. *The learner saddles a horse.*

_____ 5. *The learner separates into separate piles a mixed stack of saddles and tomatoes.*

_____ 6. *The learner writes a modern day version of 1 Corinthians 13.*

Items one, three and six include verbal indicators. A learner does not need words in order to "assemble," "saddle," and "separate."

● Now, let's look at another form of verbs used in indicators. Sometimes the verb indicates that the learner discriminates (chooses) between or among things. The learner classifies or chooses from among two or more things. For example, a learner may choose which of three stories would appeal most to preschoolers. Or he could select from a list of sentences those which use correct grammar. He separates them or discriminates among them on the basis of what he knows and understands.

■ *Which of the following statements calls for discrimination between or among things or ideas?*

_____ 1. *The learner lists five duties of a committee chairman.*

_____ 2. *The learner identifies in a list of actions those which violate the principle of "a free church in a free state."*

In item two the learner discriminates among actions. Item one calls for a verbal response. "Listing" requires writing of words. Item two calls for a discrimination form of response.

■ *Which of the following indicators suggest that the learner discriminates among things or ideas?*

_____ 1. *The learner lists the three forms of action verbs used in Indicators.*

_____ 2. *The learner studies a picture of a hospital visit and decides what the visitor did wrong.*

_____ 3. *The learner classifies a given Bible lesson plan as either inductive or deductive in approach.*

_____ 4. *The learner studies a list of indicators and checks those which represent discrimination indicators.*

All the items except one require discrimination. Number one calls for a verbal response—the learner "lists." In number 2 the learner sees something in a picture and must discriminate whether it is a correct action or an incorrect one. In number 3 the learner discriminates between inductive and deductive forms by classifying. In number 4 the learner looks at several statements and discriminates among them.

● We have looked at verbal and discrimination indicators. Now, let's look at a third form. Sometimes the action verb indicates that the learner performs some physical activity. The learner indicates he has mastered a motor skill. He may assemble, tear down, build, operate.

■ *Check the motor indicators in this list:*

_____ *1. The learner judges a debate.*

_____ *2. The learner changes the ribbon on a typewriter.*

_____ *3. The learner quotes from memory the Ten Commandments.*

Only item two calls for motor activity. In one he discriminates. In three the learner makes a verbal response. He quotes.

■ *Classify the following list of verbs according to form. Write "V" for verbal; "D" for discrimination; and "M" for motor. If the verb suggests a combination, write the combination. For example, you may write DV for some of them. Think, however, in terms of primary or most obvious kind of action.*

_____ 1. assemble   _____ 5. disassemble

_____ 2. paraphrase   _____ 6. choose

_____ 3. list   _____ 7. separate (classify)

_____ 4. select   _____ 8. ski

    With room for argument, these answers show the proper classification: M, V, V, D, and M, D, D, M.

■ *Which one word in this goal-indicator statement tells what the pupil does to prove he has learned? Underline the word.*

The learner understands the three forms of indicators. To prove he has achieved this goal, the learner classifies a list of ten indicators as verbal, discrimination, or motor.

You should have underlined the word classifies.

■ *What kind of action does "identifies examples of properly stated indicators" suggest?*

_____ 1. verbal

_____ 2. discrimination

_____ 3. motor

    You should have checked item two. In the example, the learner must discriminate among correct and incorrect examples.

2. *Indicators tell how well the learner should perform.*—Indicators tell not only what the learner will do to prove he has learned. They tell, when necessary, how well he should perform. For example, the indicator may state that the learner will achieve 80 percent accuracy. The teacher who states how well the pupil should perform commits himself to teach until the pupil achieves that level.

■ *Which two of the following goal-indicators tell exactly how well the pupil should do?*

_____ 1. *The student demonstrates knowledge of the breeds of poultry. To prove achievement of this goal, the learner classifies according to name and class, ninety-five of one hundred pictures of poultry.*

_____ 2. *The student demonstrates an attitude of concern for stream pollution in Tarrant County. To prove achievement of this goal, the learner does such things as: reports violations, organizes volunteer groups to correct problems; make proposals for stream pollution control to the city council.*

_____ 3. *The student demonstrates skill in using the breast stroke in swimming. To prove achievement of this goal, the student does such things as: swims fifty yards in two minutes using the breast stroke.*

Items one, three tell how well the learner will perform. Each answers the question, How well? Number 1 requires at least 95 percent accuracy. Number 3 calls for fifty yards in two minutes. Goal-indicators which deal with attitude, as in number 2, usually do not tell how well the student will perform. Teachers find it difficult to express "how well" in this type of goal. Number 2 does not indicate "how well" the student will perform.

● Some indicators do not specify precisely "how well?" The teacher and student may assume a requirement of one hundred percent. The indicator implies 100 percent. For example, if a statement calls for "writing the Beatitudes" we assume it means all (100 percent) of them.

The indicator should either state "how well," or imply 100 percent. An indicator never uses "some" as an expression of "how well." "Some" could mean *any* number more than one!

■ **Which of the following indicators imply 100 percent without saying so?**

_____ **1. The learner arranges in chronological order ten events in the story of redemption.**

_____ **2. The learner computes correctly nine out of ten addition problems.**

Item one implies *100 percent accuracy. It does not state a lower acceptable figure. You should have checked number 1. Number 2 calls for 90 percent accuracy.*

■ **Write the first two characteristics of an indicator:**

1. _____

2. _____

You should have answered in these or similar words: (1) They state what the learner does to prove he has learned. (2) They tell how well the learner should perform.

● Now, let's look at a third characteristic of an indicator.

3. *Sometimes the indicators describe the special conditions under which the learner will perform.*—"Conditions" mean the circumstances under which the learner responds. They describe the "givens" of the situation. [1]

Sometimes the indicator makes it obvious what the learner receives with which to work.

■ *What does the learner have to work with in this indicator:*

Given three case studies, the learner identifies the one which illustrates the proper way to make a motion.

"Given three case studies" describes the conditions. The learner has three case studies with which to work.

■ *In the following statement, the pupil receives something with which to work. It doesn't appear at first glance. See if you can find it. Underline it.*

The pupil arranges in chronological order a random list of seven events in the story of redemption.

Ask yourself, What does the learner receive with which to work? Does he prepare his own list of events? No. The teacher provides the list of events. Under those conditions, the learner arranges them. You should have underlined "a random list of seven events."

All indicators should state what the learner will do to prove he has learned. When possible and needed the indicators should also state how well and under what circumstances. [2]

---

[1] Indicators include a time limitation as a condition *only* if time is a crucial factor.

[2] One finds it difficult to specify all standards when the indicator calls for performance at the higher levels of learning. (See unit 4.)

CHECK YOUR PROGRESS

■ *Only one of the indicators in the following list includes all three elements: what the learner will do; how well; and under what conditions or circumstances. Check the indicator which contains all three.*

_____ 1. *The learner lists some of the characteristics of a good steward as described by Paul in 1 Thessalonians.*

_____ 2. *The learner identifies in a list of three paraphrases of Romans 3:23 the one which most nearly conveys the meaning in the King James Version.*

_____ 3. *The learner understands the three essential elements in repentance.*

Only item two includes all three elements: What does the learner do? He identifies in a list. How well? "The paraphrase" implies selecting the one paraphrase—or 100 percent. Under what conditions? Obviously the teacher furnishes the learner with three paraphrases. The learner does not have to make them up himself.

Number 1 tells what the learner will do. He lists. However, it does not tell how many he will list. The word "some" does not tell how well. If the learner stated any number more than one then he would meet the requirement for "some." Apparently he lists, from memory, the implied condition.

Number 3 does not tell what the learner will do to prove he has learned. We would call number 3 a goal—not an indicator.

■ *Now, write the three characteristics of an indicator.*

1. _____

2. _____

3. _____

You should have used these or similar words: (1) They state what the learner will do. (2) They tell how well the learner will perform. (3) They describe the circumstances.

■ *Study the following goal-indicator. Then answer the questions which follow it.*

The learner understands Robert's Rules of Order. To prove achievement of this goal, the learner writes the proper action a moderator should make in regard to ten given motions. He handles nine out of ten of them correctly.

1. What does the learner do to prove he understands rules of order?

_____

2. How well must he perform?

_____

3. Under what conditions does he perform?

_____

You should have answered: (1) Writes proper actions. (2) Nine out of ten. (3) Given ten motions.

You have learned the basic principles for writing goal-indicators.

Units 4 and 5 focus on an interesting aspect of indicators which can become a milestone in your training as a teacher. They deal with "levels of learning." The units will help you discover what "levels of learning" means and how this understanding can help you become a better teacher.

THE
PLANNING
PROCESS

UNIT 3

You Don't Drive a Nail with a Stick of Butter!

Why You Will Find the Study Useful:

You can apply the process presented in this
unit to design learning activities for almost
any lesson plan. Once you learn the process
you can apply it in many different situations.

What You May Expect to Learn:

Goal: A study of this unit will help
you understand the process used to
design effective learning activities.

What You Will Do to Prove You Have Achieved the Goal for This Study:

Summarize the process used to design learning
activities so as to include the three parts
of the process.

Preview of Terms Used in This Unit:

Oops! We don't believe you will need a glossary for this unit!

You will need approximately 20 minutes to complete this unit.

UNIT 3

You Don't Drive a Nail with a Stick of Butter!

Some teachers teach as if what they know about how persons learn had absolutely nothing to do with what happens in the classroom!

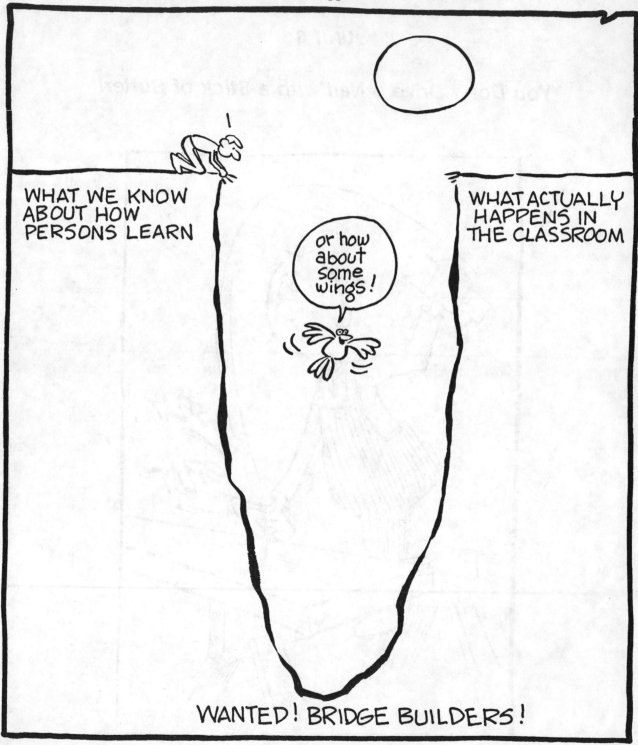

● We believe that the plan in this unit will cause you to say, "I've found it!—a better way to design learning activities! A better way to plan lessons!" By "better way," we mean an educationally sound way. We mean a way which applies in the classroom what one knows about how persons learn.

We can design learning activities which get results. The first clue to how to do it appears in the goal-indicator statement of a lesson plan. Does it contain a word like "knowledge," "understanding," "attitude," or "skill"? [1] If so, you're on your way. That word clues you in on how to select the right kinds of learning activities to reach a goal. It tells whether to use skill development activities, knowledge (memory or recall) activities, or some other kind.

Some activities lend themselves to teaching for knowledge (memory or recall). They differ as a rule from those used to teach for understanding, attitude, or skill. Other activities lend themselves to teaching for understanding. They differ as a rule from those used for the other kinds of learning, and so on.

■ *Which of the following approaches would you use to help a learner learn something by memory? (Note the four choices.)*

_____ 1. *Ask the learner to repeat the material over and over. Let him know immediately whether he is right or wrong.*

_____ 2. *Ask the learner to rewrite the material in his own words, keeping the same meaning.*

_____ 3. *Both 1 and 2.*

_____ 4. *Neither 1 nor 2.*

Item one suggests the use of drill methods. This, indeed, helps the pupil learn by memory. Drill results in knowledge. The learner recalls the facts when asked. Number 2 does little to make it possible for him to repeat from memory. It would help him understand the meaning. But as a rule drill would help the learner memorize facts. You should have checked number one.

_____

[1] This in no way implies that we should limit the number of outcomes to these four. Others include creativity, appreciation, and so on. We have selected these four as good ones with which to begin.

● Teachers and leaders need to decide whether they will teach primarily for change in knowledge, understanding, skill or attitude and values.

We know a lot about *how* persons gain knowledge; *how* learners develop understanding, attitudes, and skills. We can use certain principles of learning to help bring about *certain kinds* of learning. If we teach for understanding, it helps to use certain principles of learning to cause understanding to take place and endure.

Assume that the learning goal pinpoints *skill* as the primary learning outcome. For example: The learner demonstrates *skill* in tying seven kinds of knots. Skill means the ability to do with ease a motor act—such as typing, skiing or tying knots. The term *skill* tells the teacher-trainer that he should use those learning principles which tend to result in *skill*.

One learning principle says *a learner develops skill more easily when he sees the skill demonstrated*. We might call this the "principle of demonstration." Another says he gains skill more easily *when he practices the operation himself*. We might call this the "principle of repeated performance." Using these two principles and others, the teacher-trainer designs learning activities. He provides opportunities which permit the learner to "see the skill demonstrated" and to "practice the operation himself." In this way he applies in the classroom what he knows about how people learn skills.

73

■ *Which of the following learning activities indicates that the learner "saw the skill demonstrated"?*

_____ 1. *A group of Boy Scouts saw a film on how to tie seven different kinds of knots.*

_____ 2. *A group of Boy Scouts listened to a speech on the uses of seven different kinds of knots.*

Item two does not indicate that the Scouts saw or observed a demonstration. They could have listened to the speech and never have even seen a picture of a knot! Number 1 indicates that the Scouts saw a demonstration by means of a film. Whether the learner sees a filmed demonstration or a "live" demonstration makes little difference. The means through which one sees a demonstration has little to do with it. You should have checked number one.

So, the teacher saw the word skill *in the learning goal. The word* skill *called to mind the principle that "learners develop skills more effectively when they see the skill demonstrated." The teacher asked, "How can I use the principle of demonstration so that the learners can see a demonstration of knot tying?" This caused him to think of showing a film which showed (demonstrated) how to tie seven knots.*

74

● We may picture this sequence of thoughts in this way:

THE GOAL TELLS US WHICH PRIMARY LEARNING OUTCOME (THE KIND OF LEARNING)	THE PRIMARY OUT-COME GUIDES US TO THE LEARNING PRINCIPLES TO USE:	THE LEARNING PRINCIPLES HELP US THINK OF THE RIGHT KIND OF LEARNING ACTIVITIES
KNOWLEDGE UNDERSTANDING (SKILL) ATTITUDE	"WHEN THEY SEE THE SKILL DEMON-STRATED.	SHOW A FILM ON HOW TO TIE SEVEN KINDS OF KNOTS.

Study again the illustration before reading further. Don't rush at this point. If you grasp what the illustration says you've achieved the goal of this unit.

Now, let's expand the illustration. Let's look at another chart which shows the same sequence of ideas. You will need to study it closely in order to do the exercise which follows it. The chart presents a process which you will use later. Begin with the "learning goal" and trace the ideas step by step through the chart.

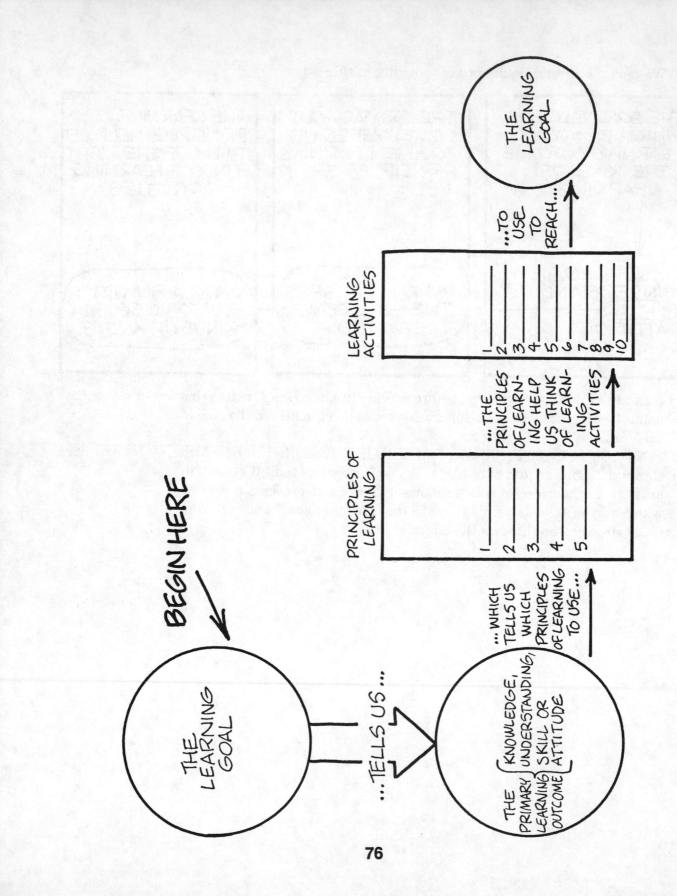

BEGIN HERE

THE LEARNING GOAL

...TELLS US...

THE PRIMARY LEARNING OUTCOME { KNOWLEDGE, UNDERSTANDING, SKILL OR ATTITUDE

...WHICH TELLS US WHICH PRINCIPLES OF LEARNING TO USE...

PRINCIPLES OF LEARNING

1
2
3
4
5

...THE PRINCIPLES OF LEARNING HELP US THINK OF LEARNING ACTIVITIES

LEARNING ACTIVITIES

1
2
3
4
5
6
7
8
9
10

...TO USE TO REACH...

THE LEARNING GOAL

76

CHECK YOUR PROGRESS

■ *Now that you have studied the two charts, decide whether these statements summarize the process described by the charts. Refer back to the charts if you desire. Notice again that you have four choices. Check one answer.*

_____ 1. *The learning goal tells us whether to teach primarily for knowledge, understanding, skill, or attitude. This gives us clues as to which learning principles to use primarily. The principles in turn help us select the right kinds of learning activities for the student to use in reaching the goal.*

_____ 2. *Learners reach learning goals by taking part in learning activities. The learning activities used to reach goals call for use of principles of learning. These principles should relate properly to the kind of learning described (the primary learning outcomes of knowledge, understanding, skill, attitude). We look at the learning goal to determine which primary learning outcomes to teach toward.*

_____ 3. *Both 1 and 2.*

_____ 4. *Neither 1 nor 2.*

Both statements describe what the charts say. You should have checked item three. Item two simply begins at the righthand side of the chart and proceeds to the left. Number 1 begins at the left and proceeds to the right.

■ *Now, try writing in your own words the planning process described in the charts.*

_____

_____

_____

_____

_____

Refer back to the preceding activity to check your answer.

Check to see that your summary includes these three parts: (1) the learning goal tells us the primary learning outcome; (2) the learning outcome tells us which principle of learning to use; and (3) the principles of learning help us think of the right kind of learning activities to use in reaching the goal. There you have it—in a nutshell.

If you comprehend this process, you are ready to proceed to a study of the guidelines or principles of learning we use to help persons know, understand, do, and feel.

**KNOWLEDGE
AND
UNDERSTANDING
OUTCOMES**

UNIT 4

Every Round Goes Higher, Higher!

Why You Will Find the Study Useful:

Pupils need to learn facts. But they need
  also to learn to apply in a useful way
  what they learn. They need to progress to
  higher "levels" of learning. The learning
  indicators you will learn to write will
  call for the level of learning the pupil
  needs. Then you can complete your lesson
  plans in keeping with the desired "level."
  And, of course, you can use the indicators
  as a basis for tests.

What You May Expect to Learn:

Goal: A study of this unit should help you
  understand the process of writing learning
  indicators (objectives) at three levels of
  learning. Knowledge (recall), comprehension,
  and application. [1]

Some Things You Will Do to Prove You Have Achieved This Goal:

* Write indicators at three levels of learning
  (knowledge, comprehension, application).
* Classify a list of indicators as to the learning
  level each suggests.
* Define the first three levels of learning related to
  knowledge and understanding.
* Define "levels of learning."
* List the first three levels of learning related to
  knowledge and understanding.

You will need approximately 45 minutes to complete this unit.

---

[1] The first three levels of learning related to knowledge and understanding. See
Taxonomy of Educational Objectives, Handbook 1: Cognitive Domain, edited by Benjamin S. Bloom, David McKay Co., New York, 1956. Used by permission.

Preview of Terms Used in This Unit:

Level of learning.—A way of expressing the degree to which an activity requires the pupil to rely upon what he has learned before. For example, learning facts suggests a low level of learning. But a pupil needs to know facts before he can solve problems with them. This unit deals with the three lower levels of learning related to knowledge and understanding: knowledge (recall), comprehension, and application. (Unit 5 will deal with three higher levels.)

Knowledge.—In this unit, knowledge means ability to recall facts and information. Recall suggests the lowest—but a worthy—level of learning.

Comprehension.—This second level of learning suggests ability to express ideas in new ways. One who comprehends can explain how one idea relates to another.

Application.—This third level of learning suggests the ability to use in a new situation something one has learned before. It suggests "transfer of learning."

UNIT 4

Every Round Goes Higher! Higher!

● It's easier to walk on level ground than to climb mountains! But sometimes we must climb mountains. Some learning tasks require more effort than others. Some activities require us to rely on something we have learned before. We learn simple things and we learn complex things. We find degrees of complexity in the knowledge and understanding we gain. Sometimes we learn facts. At other times we learn what the facts mean. Sometimes we solve complex problems. In between the simple and the complex learnings we find learning of medium difficulty.

Teachers and leaders need to decide whether a lesson plan should call for simple or complex learning. This chapter will help you decide.

■ *Let's begin by looking at two learning tasks. Which of the following tasks would you consider the simpler?*

_____ *1. The learner writes four guidelines for witnessing.*

_____ *2. In a case study on witnessing the learner identifies the witnessing guidelines the witness violated.*

Item two requires more complex thinking than item one. In number 1, the learner recalls the guidelines. Writing the guidelines tests his memory—whether he can recall facts. In number 2, the learner must not only know the guidelines for witnessing. He must recognize violations of them.

SOME LEARNING TASKS ARE MORE DIFFICULT THAN OTHERS!

● We call these differences of complexity "levels of learning." The levels of learning refer to the degree to which a person must rely on previous learning. They refer also to the complexity of thinking involved in gaining knowledge and understanding.

And where do levels of learning fit into lesson planning? Answer: *Teachers and trainers can write indicators to match the level of learning the pupil should achieve.*

If the pupil needs to recall facts, the teacher can write an indicator at that level. The pupil may need to do more than recall facts. If so, the teacher can write indicators which ask him to do more. In Unit 2, you learned to identify properly stated indicators. In this unit you will learn to identify them according to the level of learning they represent. Now, let's find out more about the levels. [1]

■ *Even without studying the levels of learning, you probably can arrange the following three indicators according to complexity. Read the three indicators. Assign the number 1 to the one which represents the lowest (simplest) learning level; number 3 to the most complex level, and so on.*

_____ *The learner writes from memory four Scripture passages to use in witnessing.*

_____ *The learner paraphrases four given verses of Scripture used in witnessing.*

_____ *The learner uses in the right way four verses of Scripture in an evangelistic visit.*

Interestingly enough, you should have listed them in order 1, 2, 3. At the lowest level, the learner writes four verses from memory. Next, by paraphrasing, he proves that he comprehends what the verses mean. Comprehending meanings requires learning at a higher level than simply writing something from memory. In number 3 the learner applies (uses) in a new situation the verses learned. He transfers to a new situation the things he has learned about use of the Scriptures.

[1] Adapted from *Taxonomy of Educational Objectives, Handbook 1: Cognitive Domain,* edited by Benjamin S. Bloom, David McKay Co., Inc., New York, 1956.

● Again, what has this to do with learning to teach and lead? Simply this: *Teachers and leaders can deliberately write goals and indicators to call for learning at whatever level the pupil needs.*

In the outcomes of knowledge and understanding we usually think of six levels. But in this unit we will deal with the first three only. Later, if you desire, you may study the other three in unit 5. Now let's preview the first three levels. [1]

1. On the lowest level the learner recalls or recognizes facts and information. He learns at the *knowledge* or memory level.

2. The learner may explain (interpret) the facts or change (translate) them into a new form (such as paraphrasing). If so, he learns at the *comprehension* level.

3. He may learn to use in new situations what he has learned. If so he learns at the level of *application.*

The ladder below shows the first three levels in order. Remember, these levels relate to the learning outcomes of knowledge and understanding. So if you want to teach for knowledge or understanding, you can use these levels to help you pinpoint the complexity of the learning desired.

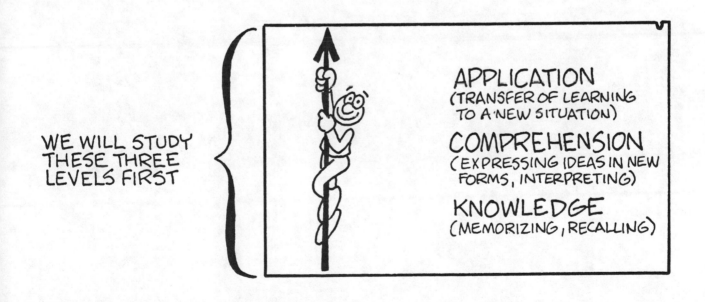

WE WILL STUDY THESE THREE LEVELS FIRST

APPLICATION (TRANSFER OF LEARNING TO A NEW SITUATION)

COMPREHENSION (EXPRESSING IDEAS IN NEW FORMS, INTERPRETING)

KNOWLEDGE (MEMORIZING, RECALLING)

[1] Adapted from *Taxonomy of Educational Objectives, Handbook 1: Cognitive Domain,* edited by Benjamin S. Bloom, David McKay Co., Inc., New York, 1956.

Teachers can learn to write indicators of goal achievement at any level of learning they choose. For example, a trainer of Sunday School teachers could simply teach facts and information about teaching. He would use an indicator which called for the learner to recall facts and information—the knowledge level. The trainer probably would want the trainee to learn to apply a given principle. If so, he would help the learner put the principle into practical use. The indicator would call for the trainee to function at the application level.

A teacher needs to ask, At what level do the pupils need to learn? Then he can phrase the indicator to reflect the desired level. Once he determines the right level, he writes an indicator at that level. Then he keeps on teaching and training until the learner reaches that level.

Let's look more closely at the first three levels of learning: knowledge, comprehension and application. (Later we will consider the three higher levels.)

1. *The knowledge level.*—The knowledge level calls for the learner to recall facts and information from memory. We sometimes call this the memory or recall level. The learner remembers facts and information he has learned before. He may recall in at least two ways: (1) He may recall the specific facts or (2) he may simply recognize the facts when he sees them. [1] If he remembers the names of the four Gospels, he simply recalls something he has learned before. He could list them if someone asked him to do so. Or, he could not recall them, but if he saw the names of the Gospels in a list of books of the Bible he could pick them out. He would simply recognize on sight the facts he learned before.

■ **Which of the following indicators call(s) for the learner to respond at the knowledge level.**

_____ **1. The learner recites John 3:16.**

_____ **2. The learner prepares a sermon on John 3:16.**

In item one the learner recalls from memory. He responds at the knowledge level. Item two calls for learning or response at a much higher level. We will consider the higher levels later in Unit 5.

---

[1] This book makes no attempt to treat all the areas dealt with under knowledge in *Taxonomy of Educational Objectives, Handbook 1, Cognitive Domain.* Readers should consult the *Taxonomy* for a detailed treatment.

■ *Which of the following indicators call(s) for learning at the knowledge level? (Note: If both are correct, check both.)*

_____ 1. *The learner writes from memory and in chronological order the names of the cities Paul visited on his first missionary journey.*

_____ 2. *In a list of names of thirty cities in the Near East, the learner identifies the cities Paul visited on his first missionary journey.*

Remember that knowledge level involves either recall from memory or the ability to recognize when one sees it previously learned material one has learned before. You should have checked both items. Both one and two represent learning at the memory or knowledge level.

■ *Which of the following indicators represent(s) learning at the knowledge level? Remember that both recall and recognition relate to knowledge.*

    _____ *1. The learner writes a research paper on "How We Got Our Bible."*

    _____ *2. The learner matches a list of versions of the Bible with a list of dates of the versions.*

In item one the learner has to do much more than recall facts. He must, of course, get the facts, but he must organize and interpret them if he writes a research paper. Therefore, it represents a much higher level of learning than knowledge. Number 2 only requires the learner to recognize facts (dates) when he sees them. He matches them with other facts he has learned. He learns at the knowledge or recall level. You should have chosen item two.

2. *The comprehension level.*—When a learner comprehends, he grasps the meaning of facts and information he has learned. Here we move into the area of understanding. A person who comprehends something can convert it or change (translate) it into new forms. Or, he can recognize a *new form* of the idea when he sees one. For example, if a learner writes Romans 3:23 in his own words (paraphrases), he learns at the comprehension level. He "translates" from one version of the Bible into his own version. Or if he looks at a paraphrase of Romans 3:23 and recognizes it as having the correct meaning, he learns at the comprehension level.

A learner may do a pantomime which "pictures" a concept or idea. We say that he "translates the idea into a new form." But the learner would need to create the pantomime himself. If he looks at a picture and makes up a title which describes it, he translates a picture idea into a verbal idea (words). He *comprehends.*

Or the learner may explain, summarize, or interpret material he has learned. If so, he learns at the comprehension level, also. For example, the learner may study a passage of Scripture and state its central truth. He summarizes what the Scripture says. He learns at the comprehension level.

He may compare or contrast ideas or viewpoints. For example, he may explain the difference Baptists and Catholics have on the purpose of baptism.

■ *Which of the following indicators call(s) for learning at the comprehension level? Note that you may choose from four alternatives, including "both" and "neither."*

_____ 1. *The learner rewrites a dictionary definition of sin, using only one-syllable words.*

_____ 2. *The learner contrasts the "turn the other cheek" teaching of Jesus with the "eye for an eye and a tooth for a tooth" teaching of the Old Testament.*

_____ 3. *Both 1 and 2.*

_____ 4. *Neither 1 nor 2.*

Let's take a close look. In number 1, the learner "translates into a new form" a definition of sin—a definition which consists of one-syllable words. In doing so, he must think through the meaning and express it in a new form. He changes the idea (translates) from one form into a new one.

In number 2, the learner interprets and explains the two viewpoints. He must recall certain facts, but he must do more. He must go to a higher level—the level of comprehension. You should have checked number 3. Both 1 and 2 call for learning at the comprehension level.

■ *Now, for more practice. Classify the following indicators. Write "Knowledge" in front of those which represent the knowledge level. Write "Comprehension" in front of those which call for comprehension.*

1. _____ *The learner draws a simple picture which illustrates "fellowship."*

2. _____ *The learner lists the characters in Julius Caesar.*

3. _____ *The learner looks at a list of characters from Shakespeare's plays and checks those from Julius Caesar.*

4. _____ *The learner interprets the meaning of the Greek word agape.*

You should have written these answers: (1) Comprehension: the learner translates a word—fellowship—into a new form—a drawing. (2) Knowledge: the learner merely recalls names. (3) Knowledge: the learner simply looks at a list and recognizes facts. (4) Comprehension: the learner explains and elaborates on an idea.

3. *The application level.*—We could nickname this level "transfer." When a learner can apply (transfer) to a new situation something he has learned before, he *applies* learning. Application means "transfer of learning." The learner can transfer to a new situation a truth or a principle, without guidance. For example, a learner may comprehend the principle that persons tend to learn better when they use more than one of the senses at the same time. He applies his learning when he uses an audiovisual learning aid. He learns a principle, then employs the principle in using the aid. Application does not mean putting into practice a great many principles and ideas to form a new complex product. *It means usually the application of one or a very few principles.*

In another example, a doctor may face a counseling problem. He deliberately *uses* the guideline "let the other person talk." He practices at the application level. He makes practical use of something he has learned. Conducting a complete counseling session would mean the application of *many* guidelines. But application refers to use of one or a few at a time.

Remember that application means putting into practice. Application can also mean recognition of application of an idea or principle. The pupil may not apply it himself, but given some examples, he may recognize which example applies the idea. A learner may apply a principle of grammar by correcting an incorrect sentence. But he may also look at several sentences and pick out the one which applies the principle. In both cases he applies what he learns.[1]

---

[1] Some authorities would place recognition of examples at the comprehension level. We prefer to classify it as application.

■ *Which of the following indicators call(s) for learning at the application level? (Notice again the four choices.)*

      _____ *1. The learner lists three forms of church government.*

      _____ *2. The learner matches three forms of church government with the names of religious groups which practice them.*

      _____ *3. Both 1 and 2.*

      _____ *4. Neither 1 nor 2.*

Excuse this sneaky exercise. Neither represents learning at the application level. The learner only recalls (knowledge level). You should have checked number four.

■ *Which of the following suggest(s) application by recognition of examples?*

      _____ *1. The learner identifies in a case study the person who practiced "turning the other cheek."*

      _____ *2. The learner identifies in case studies the counseling principles violated.*

      _____ *3. Both 1 and 2.*

      _____ *4. Neither 1 nor 2.*

You should have checked item three. Both call for recognition of examples of application of learning. Number 2 simply approaches the matter from the negative point of view.

■ *Which of the following indicators call(s) for learning at the application level?*

_____ 1. *Given a list of the names of the books of the Bible and a list of division names according to the Jewish tradition, the learner classifies the books according to division.*

_____ 2. *The learner uses correctly the "What-would-you-do?" case study method.*

_____ 3. *Both 1 and 2.*

_____ 4. *Neither 1 nor 2.*

Number 1 requires only the recognition and recall of facts. The learner recalls which books of the Bible belong to which division according to the Jewish tradition. The learner simply recognizes which names belong to certain divisions. He does not have to think about meanings. Number 2 requires the learner to apply in a demonstration the guidelines for use of the case study. You should have checked number two.

■ *For more practice, classify these indicators as "comprehension" level or "application" level.*

1. _____ *A learner rewrites an incorrect sentence so that its verb agrees with the subject in number.*

2. _____ *A learner defines in his own words the terms verb and subject.*

3. _____ *3. A learner figures the length of the side of a right triangle using a mathematical formula.*

You should have checked items one and three. In number 1 the pupil applies rules of grammar to a new situation. In number 3 the pupil applies a formula to a new problem. In number 2 the pupil defines in "his own words"—the comprehension level.

CHECK YOUR PROGRESS

■ *Now, for review, write the level of learning each of the following indicators represents.*

1. _____ **The learner writes in his own words the definitions of ten theological terms.**

2. _____ **The learner lists the names of the kings of Judah.**

3. _____ **The learner matches the names of the kings of Israel with the names of the contemporary prophets.**

4. _____ **The learner arranges a preschool department in keeping with the open space requirements.**

Numbers 2 and 3 require only that the learner recall or recognize information. You should have written "knowledge" in blanks 2 and 3. In number 2 the learner recalls from memory. In number 3 he simply recognizes facts when he sees them. In number 1 the learner does more than recall and parrot back someone else's words. He defines in his own words. You should have written comprehension in the first blank. The fourth statement suggests application. The learner applies the "open space principle" as he arranges a preschool department.

■ *Now, in the chart below, write the first three levels of learning related to knowledge and understanding. Write the lowest level in the bottom blank (no. 1). Then define in your own words each level.*

LEVELS OF LEARNING	DEFINITION
3.	
2.	
1.	

You could have used these or similar words. 3. Application: transfer of learning to a new situation. 2. Comprehension: translation into new forms; explanation; interpretation. 1. Knowledge: recall or recognition of facts and information.

This completes a study of the first three levels of learning: knowledge, comprehension and, application. A study of these three levels should help you a great deal in planning lessons. Unit 5 deals with the other three. They call for learning at even higher levels. If you found this study helpful, you may want to study also Unit 5 which follows.

UNIT 5

Every Round Goes *Even* Higher!

Why You Will Find This Study Useful:

The learning indicators you will learn to
write will enable you to prepare lesson plans
which call for the pupil to learn at higher
levels of learning. And of course you can
use the indicators as a basis for tests.

What You May Expect to Learn:

Goal: A study of this unit should help you
understand the process of writing learning
indicators (objectives) at the three highest
levels of learning: analysis, synthesis, and
evaluation. [1]

Some Things You Will Do to Prove You Have Achieved This Goal:

Indicators:

* Write indicators at the three highest levels
   of learning: analysis, synthesis, and evaluation.
* Classify a list of indicators as to the level
   of learning each suggests.
* Define the three highest levels of learning
   related to understanding.
* List the three highest levels of learning
   related to understanding.
* List the three highest levels of learning
   related to understanding.

You will need approximately 40 minutes to complete this unit.

_____

[1] The three highest levels of learning related to understanding. Added to the three
levels in Unit 4, they complete the six levels in *Taxonomy of Educational Objectives,
Handbook 1: Cognitive Domain,* op. cit.

Preview of Terms Used in This Unit:

Analysis.—The level of learning at which the pupil breaks material down into its parts or solves problems in a systematic way. For example, a pupil outlines a book or predicts what effects a new law may have on gambling.

Synthesis. The level of learning at which the pupil puts parts together to form something new. He may write a newspaper article or a new lesson plan.

Evaluation.—The level of learning at which the pupil judges the value of something based on certain standards. For example, a pupil may decide which of three Sunday School lesson plans would best meet the needs of senior adults.

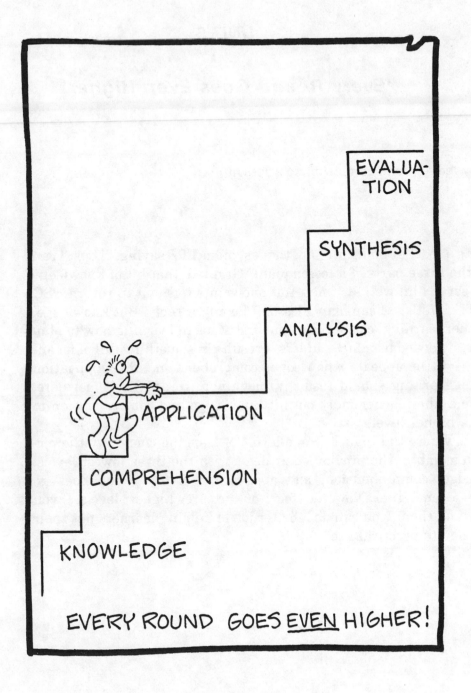

EVALUA-
TION

SYNTHESIS

ANALYSIS

APPLICATION

COMPREHENSION

KNOWLEDGE

EVERY ROUND GOES <u>EVEN</u> HIGHER!

UNIT 5

"Every Round Goes Even Higher!"

Knowledge alone cannot make a lesson plan!

● Imagine a teacher going around "the rest of his life" saying, "Look, I can name the three parts of a lesson plan!" Granted, that bit of knowledge would serve him well at times. But one wants to shout in return, "SO WHAT!" "Well, so I can plan a lesson!" he might reply. But knowledge, plus other learning, can serve as the first steps in learning how to plan lessons. Knowledge of facts, unless it results in something full of meaning, has little appeal. Knowledge, comprehension, and application levels of learning should result in meaningful products. Somewhere, sometime, the teacher must put his knowledge and comprehension to use at a higher level.

That's where the highest three levels of learning come into the picture. Remember, the previous unit dealt with the three lowest levels: knowledge, comprehension, and application. Every round does go higher—even higher! Now, let's focus on the three highest levels. If you understand them, you can do a better job of helping learners put their knowledge to practical use.

The following "ladder" shows all six levels related to knowledge and understanding. This unit deals with the top three. Read the chart and the definitions to get a preview of the unit.

THIS UNIT WILL FOCUS ON THE THREE HIGHEST LEVELS.

EVALUATION
(JUDGING VALUE BASED ON STANDARDS)

SYNTHESIS
(CREATING SOMETHING NEW BY PUTTING PARTS TOGETHER)

ANALYSIS
(BREAKING A COMMUNICATION DOWN INTO ITS PARTS)

APPLICATION

COMPREHENSION

KNOWLEDGE

The three highest levels of learning in the area of understanding we call (1) analysis, (2) synthesis, (3) and evaluation.

These terms may seem complex at first. But they will take on meaning as you progress through this unit. Remember, we study these levels in order to write goal-indicators at a level where learning becomes worthwhile.

"I'M SURE YOU WILL ENJOY YOUR VISIT WITH WHINGDING. HE CAN SAY THE MULTIPLICATION TABLES BACKWARDS IN FOUR MINUTES!"

4. *The level of analysis.*—At the analysis level, the pupil breaks a subject down into its parts. He analyzes it to see what makes it tick. He looks at something rather complex and finds out how it is organized. A pupil might prepare an outline of a book of the Bible. In doing so he breaks the book down into its parts. He finds out the book's organization scheme. He produces a clear outline picture of the book. For example, a pupil could study the book of Galatians and discover and write down Paul's "outline." The outline would arrange the ideas so as to mean something to the learner.

One also analyzes when he prepares such things as flow charts to show how ideas or actions relate to one another. For example, a pupil could do a chart showing how a bill becomes law. He could "trace" the bill from the time a legislator presents it until it becomes law. In doing so, the pupil would break the process down into its parts.

■ **Which of the following indicators represent(s) learning at the analysis level? (Note the four choices.)**

_____ **1. The learner outlines the book of Job.**

_____ **2. The learner draws an organization chart showing relationships in the Parent-Teacher Association.**

_____ **3. Both 1 and 2.**

_____ **4. Neither 1 nor 2.**

Both one and two represent analysis. In item one the learner studies carefully the book of Job to discover its organization structure. Then he divides and subdivides the material into a meaningful sequence of ideas. In number 2, the learner analyzes the work of the Parent-Teacher Association. He discovers relationships among persons and groups in relation to their duties. Then he expresses them in a diagram or chart. He breaks the whole into its parts. You should have checked number three.

105

● Analysis also involves anything a person does to solve problems. It calls for systematic thinking about problems and finding answers. It calls for solving of problems in a systematic way. [1] A systematic approach to problem solving, includes these steps: (1) State the problem. (2) Gather facts. (3) Fit the facts together to discover how they relate. (4) Suggest possible solutions. (5) Choose the better solutions.

As an example, one study group worked on the problem, How can we improve our church visitation program? The question became a trial statement of the problem. They gathered facts: How many people visit now? What excuses do people make? What does the church do to get people to visit?

Then they put the facts together. For example, the fact the church did not provide a nursery. That fact seemed to relate to the fact that few mothers of young children took part. Such fitting together of facts suggested such answers as "Provide for care of young children on visitation days." After weighing several solutions, they chose the better ones and put them into effect. In the process, they found out that the problem was not "How can we improve our visitation program." It was "How can we develop concern for the spiritual needs of people in our town?" With this new insight, they began the problem-solving process all over again.

■ *Does the following item call for analysis through problem solving?*

The learner leads a church council to study enrollment of the Sunday School classes. They study the prospect lists. Based on what they found out, they determined to add six new classes for adults and two for youth.

_____ **Yes**

_____ **No**

The council gathered data, fit the facts together, and came to a conclusion based on the data. They did use the problem solving approach. You should have checked yes.

---

[1] John Dewey equated learning witn problem solving. He popularized the systematic approach to problem solving.

■ *Which of the following indicators call(s) for learning at the analysis level? (Note the four choices.)*

_____ *1. The learner demonstrates three ways to use a flipchart in teaching.*

_____ *2. The learner views a videotaped teaching demonstration and reconstructs the teacher's lesson plans.*

_____ *3. Both 1 and 2.*

_____ *4. Neither 1 nor 2.*

In number 1, the learner uses (applies) the principles for using flipcharts. He learns at the application level. (See unit 4). In number 2, the learner breaks the demonstration into its parts. He gets the facts, and finally reconstructs the teacher's lesson plan. The learner learns at the analysis level. You should have checked number 2.

■ *Study these two indicators. Which calls for response at the analysis level?*

_____ *1. The learner diagrams a sentence.*

_____ *2. The learner describes the form of a given piece of music.*

_____ *3. Both 1 and 2.*

_____ *4. Neither 1 nor 2.*

You should have checked item three. To diagram a sentence, the student breaks it down into its parts. To describe the forms of a piece of music, the student analyzes the movements and discovers their organization pattern.

107

5. *The synthesis level.*—Don't let the word synthesis throw you! It means that the learner puts the parts together to form something new. This level calls for the learner to produce a new creative piece of work. The learner combines ideas to form new ideas or products. He may teach a lesson or write a script for a drama. He may devise a new way to classify things, or devise a plan for research. He may write a poem or make a speech, which he has planned.

In synthesis the learner pulls from all he knows and understands about a subject. He uses it to produce a new product.

Pastors function at this level when they prepare a new sermon. They bring together (synthesize) all they know and understand about forms of sermons, and methods of Bible interpretation. They apply what they understand about sermon objectives. The sermon becomes a new piece of work—a creative and original product. It reflects the many facets of sermon preparation that make for a good sermon.

■ **Which of the following indicators reflect(s) the synthesis level? (Note the four choices.)**

_____ **1. The learner constructs a sentence outline of a class lecture.**

_____ **2. The learner writes a lesson plan.**

_____ **3. Both 1 and 2.**

_____ **4. Neither 1 nor 2.**

In number 2 the learner combines in a new lesson plan all the parts in a lesson plan. A lesson plan includes goals and indicators, learning activities and aids, and some form of testing. The learner synthesizes all the parts into a new, original product. You should have checked number 2. Number 1 suggests learning at the analysis level. The learner discovers the sequence of ideas in a lecture.

108

■ *Does the indicator below call for response on the synthesis level?*

The learner divides a city map into sections according to The Census Taker's Guidebook.

_____ **Yes**

_____ **No**

The learner in this case has not only learned how to take a census. He has applied what he has learned. But he has not developed a new, creative approach. Someone else developed The Census Taker's Guidebook. You should have checked no.

■ *Does this indicator call for synthesis?*

The learner, given a data sheet, develops a new plan for taking a church census.

_____ **Yes**

_____ **No**

The "new plan" suggests synthesis. You should have checked yes.

● 6. *The evaluation level.*—In this highest level of learning the learner judges the value of something in the light of its purpose. He finds out whether something meets certain standards. One learner observed a teacher teaching a lesson. Then he rated the teacher on a scale of one to ten in the light of given standards. He rated the teacher on how well he used audiovisual aids, and so on.

■ **Which of the following indicators call(s) for learning at the evaluation level? (Note the four choices.)**

_____ 1. **Given a list of job requirements for a church staff position, and three data sheets from prospective staff members, the learner determines the best person for the job.**

_____ 2. **The learner gives a ten-minute speech on "The Results of Delay."**

_____ 3. **Both 1 and 2.**

_____ 4. **Neither 1 nor 2.**

Does number 1 suggest a list of standards? Yes, the job requirements suggest standards. Does the learner place the standards up against some given data? Yes, the data sheets. You should have checked item one. Number 2 calls for response at the synthesis level. The learner creates a new speech.

■ *Does this indicator call for response at the evaluation level?*

The learner chooses from three units of study the one best suited for preschoolers.

_____ Yes

_____ No

In this situation the learner thinks in terms of what preschoolers need and can do. He then uses what he has learned as standards by which to judge the value of the units. You should have checked yes.

111

CHECK YOUR PROGRESS

■ *Now, by way of review, write in the blanks at the lefthand side the level of learning for each of these indicators. They represent the highest three levels only: analysis, synthesis, and evaluation.*

1. _____ *The learner chooses, from three floor plans, the one which best meets the needs of senior adults.*

2. _____ *The learner devises a new floor plan for the church school building.*

3. _____ *The learner studies a patient's medical record and prescribes the right treatment.*

Number 1 suggests evaluation level. The needs of senior adults provide the standards against which the learner, judges the value of the three floor plans. Number 2 suggests synthesis level. To do a new floor plan, the learner thinks of many things—enrollment trends, costs, age-group needs, and so on. His new floor plan results from a "synthesis" of all these facets. Number 3 calls for learning at the analysis level. The learner follows a systematic problem-solving approach to decide on the right treatment.

■ *In this unit you have studied the last three levels of learning related to understanding. The chart below shows the first three levels you studied in Unit 4. Complete the chart by writing in and defining the last three levels.*

LEVELS OF LEARNING   **DEFINITION**

	LEVELS OF LEARNING	DEFINITION
	6.	
	5.	
	4.	
	3. Application	Applying learning to a new situation
	2. Comprehension	Translating (changing) into new forms, explaining.
	1. Knowledge	Memorizing, recalling

To check your answers, see the chart at the beginning of this unit.

113

■ *Now, for further practice, match the items shown below. This activity includes all six levels. Give it a try. The column at the left includes seven sample indicators calling for various levels of learning. In these samples, the indicators relate to the topic "Lesson Planning." Match the sample indicators with the level of learning shown at the right.*

_____ 1. The learner writes a lesson plan based on 1 Corinthians 13.

_____ 2. The learner lists the three elements in a lesson plan.

_____ 3. The learner classifies a list of indicators according to the level of learning each suggests.

_____ 4. The learner shows how to use a learning aid in which pupils see, hear, and touch at the same time.

_____ 5. Given five lesson plans the learner determines the planning approach each uses.

_____ 6. Given a lesson plan including a goal-indicator statement, the learner determines the extent to which the learning activities support the goal.

_____ 7. The learner develops a new approach to lesson planning.

a. **EVALUATION**

b. **SYNTHESIS**

c. **ANALYSIS**

d. **APPLICATION**

e. **COMPREHENSION**

f. **KNOWLEDGE**

With some room for argument, the probable order is as follows: 1. b; 2. f; 3. d or e; 4. d; 5. c; 6. a; 7. b. In theory each level involves all the levels below it. For example, analysis activities require the use of knowledge, comprehension, and application. For this reason one cannot draw distinct lines between the levels.

114

■ *In the blanks below write the level of learning of each indicator.*

1. _____ The learner shows how to use advance organizers in teaching.

2. _____ The learner writes a new church constitution.

3. _____ The learner writes, in order, the Ten Commandments.

4. _____ The learner writes in his own words the Preamble to the Constitution of the United States.

5. _____ The learner judges a news article on the basis of readability level, interest, outline, and proper use of grammar.

6. _____ The learner outlines the book of Job.

7. _____ The learner explains the difference between salvation and conversion.

Check your answers with these: 1. application; 2. synthesis; 3. knowledge; 4. comprehension; 5. evaluation; 6. analysis; 7. comprehension.

The teacher-trainer should become aware of the levels of learning. He should seek to state indicators clearly and to reflect the desired level of learning.

This unit completes the treatment of goals and indicators. Units 6 through 9 will help you create learning activities in keeping with lesson goals.

UNIT 6

Everybody Ought to Know—Something!

(Guidelines and Principles for Teaching for Knowledge)

Why You Will Find This Study Useful:

Many times you will need to teach and train
    so that pupils gain knowledge—ability to
    recall facts and information.

The learning activities you will learn to design
    in this unit will help you teach and train for
    knowledge.

What You May Expect to Learn:

Goal: A study of this unit should help you understand
    the process of designing learning activities for use
    in teaching and training for knowledge.

Some Things You Will Do to Prove You Have Achieved This Goal:

* Design learning activities which use
      the principles of learning (or guidelines) related
      to teaching for knowledge.
* State the guidelines or principles of learning
      used in a given learning activity.
* Recall the six guidelines for use in teaching and
      training for knowledge. [1]

You will need approximately 1 hour and 30 minutes to complete this
unit.

---

[1] This unit presents only six of the many guidelines or principles of learning which in
a special way relate to knowledge as a learning outcome. The principles do not apply
solely to knowledge as an outcome. They also prove effective in teaching and training
for other outcomes.

Active response.—Anything a pupil *does* which involves him personally in the learning process.

Overt response.—An active response which another person may observe in a pupil.

Covert response.—An active response in which the pupil acts mentally but does nothing which others can observe.

Advance organizer.—An activity which enables the pupil to see in advance the total organization of what follows. It may also fix in advance the pupil's *intent* to learn. We fix in advance the intent to learn when we say such things as "listen for" or "look for" six kinds of advance organizers.

Knowledge of results.—The realization on the part of the pupil as to whether he has made the correct response.

UNIT 6

Everybody Ought to Know—Something!
(Learning Activities to Help Learners Gain Knowledge)

● Try multiplying 789 by 853—but don't rely upon anything you *know*! Everybody ought to know—SOMETHING!

Learners need knowledge to prepare them for learning at higher levels (remember the levels of learning?). Learning at higher levels requires that a learner reach back at will and pull forward the knowledge (facts and information) he needs to solve problems.

Learners need knowledge because knowledge can affect attitude. People sometimes exclaim, "Well! I just didn't know!" They mean that new knowledge changed their attitude or mind-set. Knowledge affects understanding and skills. (Remember "diffusion of learning," Unit 1?)

Knowledge appears as the lowest level of learning in the levels you studied in Units 4 and 5. But don't make the mistake of calling knowledge—facts and information—unimportant. "Low level" does not mean an unworthy level.

When learners need to gain knowledge, the teacher asks: Which principles of learning, when applied, tend to help learners gain knowledge? The use of these principles in teaching will make learning more certain.

Read carefully the following six guidelines or principles. The list shows you "in advance" the principles which in a special way apply to gaining knowledge. They appear in an order of importance suggested by several educators. Many other guidelines also apply but these seem to play a special role in teaching for knowledge.

1. Involve the learner in activities which call for active response.

2. Provide activities in which the learner uses more than one of the *senses* at the same time.

3. Provide activities in which the learner uses advance organizers. (They see in advance the total organization pattern of the information or they establish in advance their learning intent.)

4. Provide for immediate knowledge of results.

5. Involve learner in numerous and varied activities related to the same goal.

6. Provide novel activities in regard to the information.

Everybody ought to know something!
Try multiplying these two numbers . . .

... BUT DON'T RELY ON
ANY FACTS YOU KNOW!

■ *Now read the list again. This time underline a key word which sets each principle apart from the others. This activity will help you remember the guidelines! Do not read further until you underline the words.*

You probably underlined these words: active, senses, advance, results, varied, and novel. You may have chosen others. You have responded actively in learning these six guidelines by choosing and underlining key words. Thus, you have already practiced what guideline number 1 teaches!

■ *Now, use the key words below as cues to recall the guidelines. Beside each word write in your own words the guideline it calls to mind. You do not have to use exact wording. Look at the first one as an example. Do not look at the list above as you do the exercise. Try to recall.*

Key Word	Explanation
1. active	Involve the pupil in activities in which he responds actively.
2. senses	
3. advance	
4. results	
5. varied	
6. novel	

Now check your answers with the list of principles on the preceding page.

● The section which follows presents one at a time the six guidelines or principles related to gaining knowledge. Others have proven helpful, but these six apply in a special way.

1. *Involve learners in activities which call for him to respond actively.*—One teacher asked the pupils to *write* the names of the fifty states. Another asked the pupils to check in a list of responsibilities those which a class president should perform. In both cases the learners responded actively. One *wrote* what he recalled; the other *checked* items in a list.

Learners tend to gain knowledge when they respond in an active way. This principle means that the learner should make a response which in some way requires mental activity

He may respond either overtly or covertly. If he makes an overt response, the teacher can observe the response. The teacher may watch the learner respond, or she may look at something he did.

Covert response means the pupil acts mentally but does not do anything which others can observe. He keeps it to himself. But in both cases the learner responds in an active way.

■ *Classify the following active responses as overt (O) or covert (C).*

_____ 1. Arranging word strips in chronological order on a clingchart.

_____ 2. Reading aloud an outline.

_____ 3. Thinking, What shall I do next?

_____ 4. Classifying this list of responses.

One could observe a pupil making the overt (observable) responses in one, two, and four. Three calls for covert response. The pupil does nothing which we can observe.

121

● The principle of active responding applies also to gaining understanding and to developing attitudes and skills. But it plays a special role in helping persons gain knowledge.

■ *Which of these learning activities involves the greatest amount of active response on the part of the learner?*

_____ 1. *A learner listens to a teacher read in chronological order ten historical events.*

_____ 2. *A learner arranges in chronological order a random list of ten historical events.*

In item one the learner may make no active response whatever in regard to the historical events. He may work arithmetic problems or go sailing as he "listens." Unless he mentally does something with the events as he listens, he does not respond actively at all. In number 2, the learner thinks about the order of the events. He makes covert decisions which he expresses overtly as he handles and puts in order the facts. You should have checked number two.

● In summary, use activities like the following to call for the learner to respond actively:

1. Ask the learner to write or recite something over and over.

2. Ask the learner to choose items from a list.

3. Involve him in rearranging items in a list.

4. Let him work a puzzle.

5. Ask him to match items in one list with items in another.

2. *Provide activities in which the learner uses more than one of the senses at the same time.*—A teacher may ask the pupils to arrange word strips in a chart. They see and touch at the same time. A learner who eats a piece of fruit sees, tastes, and smells at the same time.

Learners tend to gain knowledge when they use more than one of the senses at the same time. This and other principles of learning represent "rules of thumb." Certain other factors, such as intelligence and the subject studied, cause this principle to apply more to one person than to another. For example, for some learners *sound* may in fact hinder the visual aspect of a film. As a rule, however, the use of more than one of the senses at the same time results in better learning.

Learners have five senses: sight, hearing, touch, taste, and smell. Often one of the senses "fills in" information left out by the others.

■ *If you received orally the command, "Fold the paper in half at the middle," which of the following shows the correct response? (Note the four answers.)*

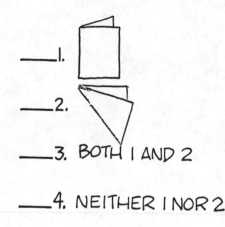

_____1.

_____2.

_____3. BOTH 1 AND 2

_____4. NEITHER 1 NOR 2

Obviously both show papers folded in half at the middle. You should have checked item three. The instructions failed to tell whether to fold the paper horizontally or diagonally. A picture of the folded paper would have shown what the oral instructions left out.

THE SAME WORDS MAY MEAN DIFFER-
ENT THINGS TO DIFFERENT PEOPLE!

The same words may mean different things to different people. The teacher prevents mistakes in communication by showing and telling at the same time.

■ **Which of the following activities call for use of more than one of the senses at the same time?**

_____ 1. **Listening to a recording**

_____ 2. **Attending a motion picture**

_____ 3. **Analyzing a chart**

_____ 4. **Assembling a bicycle**

_____ 5. **Eating a chicozapote**

Under ordinary conditions, two, four, and five would require use of more than one of the senses. Motion pictures as a rule use both sight and sound. Assembling a bicycle calls for sight, sound and touch. Eating a chicozapote, whatever that is, would involve all five senses at the same time.

■ *Which of the following excerpts from a lesson plan involves more than one of the senses at the same time? Remember to look for the use of more than one of the senses.*

_____ 1. *Display on a table these aids to Bible study: a Bible dictionary, a concordance, a one-volume commentary, and two or three modern translations of the Bible. Then distribute the items to pupils as you explain their purposes.*

_____ 2. *Play for the group a recorded interview with a medical doctor on the "Four effects of drugs on the mental health of users."*

_____ 3. *Arrange in random order on a clingchart six word strips showing the levels of learning. Ask pupils to rearrange them in order of complexity.*

Items one and three call for use of more than one of the senses. Number 1 involves sight—they see the books. They hear the teacher explain their uses. They touch the books as they handle them. In number 2, the learner hears only. In number 3 the learner sees the word strips and touches them as he rearranges them. You should have checked numbers one and three.

Lesson-plan writers can deliberately involve more than one of the senses in a learning activity.

● Provide activities such as the following to involve learners in the use of more than one of the senses at the same time:

1. Ask them to view a motion picture.

2. Present a chart and explain it orally—or permit the learner to do so.

3. Show a filmstrip with narration.

4. Arrange for learners to handle objects.

5. Involve learners in the use of drama.

6. Allow learners to assemble and take apart articles.

● 3. *Provide activities in which the learner uses advance organizers.*[1]— One teacher showed a chart of goals for the next unit of study. The chart organized the subject matter in advance. The learners read all the goals *in advance*. Another teacher asked the pupils to listen for the things that happened to Paul on his first missionary journey. She then read aloud the passage. She helped organize in advance the learner's *intent* to learn. They intended to learn the events.

Learners tend to gain knowledge when they use advance organizers.

We can apply this principle in two ways: Learners learn better (1) when they decide in advance what they intend to learn, and (2) when they see in advance the total organization pattern of the information. Now what does all of that mean? First, note that we have said two things: Persons learn better (1) when they establish in advance their learning intent, and (2) when they see the total organization pattern in advance. Let's consider these points separately.

(1) *When they establish in advance their intent to learn.*—We may use advance organizers to establish learning intent at the beginning of a study. Teachers use various techniques to fix in advance the learners' intent to learn. Sometimes a statement of learning goals and indicators fixes their intent. They "intend" to achieve the learning which the goals and indicators express. But a much simpler use of the principle has found its way into modern teaching methods. Study this example:

A teacher read aloud Psalm 119. Before reading it *she asked the pupils to listen for words which mean the same thing as "God's Word."* She fixed *in advance* the learning intent. The pupil's intent was to listen for synonyms. They did not know how many they would hear, but they knew in advance the things for which to listen. Their intent led them to find out which words the psalmist used to mean "God's Word."

Study this example:

A teacher read aloud a story from a newspaper. Before reading the story he asked one group of pupils to listen for the events which led to the crisis. He asked another to listen for the pros and cons of the solution to the crisis. The teacher read. The pupils became alert as the teacher told of events and arguments for and against the solutions. Then the teacher called for reports. They intended to find out the events, and the arguments for and against the solution. They fixed their learning intent in advance.

The *listening team* method has its roots in this principle.

---

[1] Some research has shown that the use of advance organizers aids learning; other research shows that it does not. This writer prefers to accept the principle as stated.

■ *Which of the following three learning activities establish(es) learning intent in advance?*

_____ *1. A Sunday School teacher asked one student to read aloud 1 John 1:1–5. The teacher asked other students to listen for the "senses" through which the writer of the passage had known Christ.*

_____ *2. A teacher gave a "completion" test at the end of a unit of study.*

_____ *3. A teacher gave the students at the beginning of a unit an "open book" test; the students looked up the answers.*

Items one and three fixed learning intent in advance. In number one the students "listened for" in order to fulfill an assignment. In number 3 the test questions presented before study began fixed in advance the learning intent. Number 2 occurred at the end of the session so we could hardly call it an advance organizer.

130

■ *Which of the following learning activities use(s) an advance organizer to establish learning intent?*

_____ *1. At the beginning of the session, display a chart showing the "three meanings of love."*

_____ *2. Present the film,* Learning to Sail. *Ask group members to note the names of the parts of a sailing rig. Then call for reports.*

_____ *3. Both 1 and 2.*

_____ *4. Neither 1 nor 2.*

You should have checked item two. Item one illustrates the use of advance organizers—but not to establish learning intent. Only number 2 fixes in advance the learner's intentions. He will listen for the names of the parts of a sailing rig. He will remember such terms as gaff, boom, sheet.
We may use advance organizers in another way.

131

● (2) *When they see in advance the total organization pattern.*—To help you comprehend what this means, let's do an experiment. *Read all of these directions before you begin.* On page 134 appears a design or arrangement of several dots (don't look yet!). You are to look at the page for only *four seconds.* Time yourself or have someone else time you. (Remember—only four seconds. If you look longer you make the experiment invalid.) After you look at the dots, estimate the number of dots you think you saw. Write the number in the margin of this page. Ready? Go!

Now, do the same thing but look at page 140. (Remember—only four seconds. If you look longer you make the experiment invalid.) How many dots do you think you saw? Record your estimate in the margin of this page. You probably came closer to the correct answer when you saw the dots on page 134. Your mind sought out an organization pattern to which you could cling. In the same manner, we perceive organization patterns among facts and ideas. This tends to aid memory.

Try the experiment on a friend. You can control the time, allowing him to look only four seconds.

In teaching the elements in long-range planning, a leader began a session by listing on the chalkboard these elements: purpose, philosophy, objectives, organization, personnel, facilities, finances, evaluation. Then he began to deal with the items one at a time. Students saw in advance the names of the eight elements. They knew in advance the subjects with which the entire course would deal. They could then relate to the outline the learnings which they acquired later.

■ *Which of the following represent(s) use of the principle of advance organizers in such a way that the learner sees in advance the total organization plan?*

_____ 1. *To begin the unit, ask the pupils to read the ten lesson titles on the contents page.*

_____ 2. *Ask pupils to make a sentence outline of chapter 3.*

_____ 3. *Both 1 and 2.*

_____ 4. *Neither 1 nor 2.*

You should have checked item one. Pupils see the topics and get a glimpse of things to come. In number 2 the pupil does not see the outline in advance. He must make it himself. This suggests a very worthwhile thing to do but it does not call for use of advance organizers.

1 ●

2 ● ●

3 ● ● ●

4 ● ● ● ●

5 ● ● ● ● ●

6 ● ● ● ● ● ●

7 ● ● ● ● ● ● ●

● Sometimes a summary statement studied or read during the first part of a study can convey a bird's-eye view of an entire unit of study. It serves as an advance organizer.

■ *Read the statement which follows. Pupils studied it at the beginning of a unit on teacher training. Circle key words which suggest topics for later study in the unit.*

Planning for learning requires statement of goals. The goals suggest the primary learning outcome and the subject. We measure the achievement of goals with indicators which state what the pupil will do to prove he has learned. The primary learning outcome tells the kind of learning involved—knowledge, understanding, skill, attitude. These outcomes point toward principles of learning which one may put to work in learning activities. After the pupil achieves the learning goals by taking part in learning activities, we evaluate the results. We use the indicators as standards of achievements.

You probably circled the same topics you study in this book: goals, indicators, primary learning outcomes, principles of learning, learning activities, and testing or evaluation. You now have in advance a bird's-eye view of lesson planning.

■ *Now, let's review once again the uses of advance organizers to fix learning intent. The list below includes examples of both ways to use advance organizers. Check those which fix in advance the learning intent.*

_____ 1. *To begin the study display a list of the names of the bones in the human body.*

_____ 2. *Ask pupils to read silently the Preamble to the Constitution. Ask them to list the reasons for a Constitution as they read.*

_____ 3. *Divide the class into two teams. Ask team one to listen during the lecture for the names of cities involved. Ask team two to listen for the kinds of problems cities face.*

_____ 4. *On the chalkboard write the three-point outline of the lesson. Then call on three persons to speak for five minutes on an assigned point.*

You should have checked two and three. Each tells the learner the items for which to search. Neither shows them a list in advance (as in one and four).

■ *A teacher in a course in using learning aids displayed this chart at the beginning of a unit of study. Does it call for the use of an advance organizer?*

Eight Values of Learning Aids

1.   5.

2.   6.

3.   7.

4.   8.

Did the chart serve as an advance organizer?

_____ *1. Yes*

_____ *2. No*

The chart did serve as an advance organizer. The teacher displayed it at the first of a session. The students knew they would learn about eight values of learning aids.

137

■ *Which of the following reasons explains why we would think of the previous chart an advance organizer:*

_____ 1. *The chart listed for them eight values of learning aids.*

_____ 2. *The chart did not list the eight values but established intent to learn what the eight values are.*

The chart did not list the eight values. The chart did suggest that the learners would learn about eight values. At the beginning they did not know them. But in their minds they prepared themselves to listen for the eight values. You should have checked number 2.

■ *Now, for review, write the first three guidelines or principles presented up to this point.*

1. _____
   _____
2. _____
   _____
3. _____
   _____

Check the preceding pages in this chapter for answers.

138

● You can make use of "advance organizers" by involving learners in activities such as these:

1. Ask them to study the contents page of a book.

2. Call for teams to listen for certain things during a lecture.

3. Ask "watching teams" to watch for certain things in a film.

4. At the first of a unit of study, ask each student to read a summary of the lesson.

5. Lead the learners in review-preview activities.

6. In advance, show objects which suggest the topics with which a unit deals.

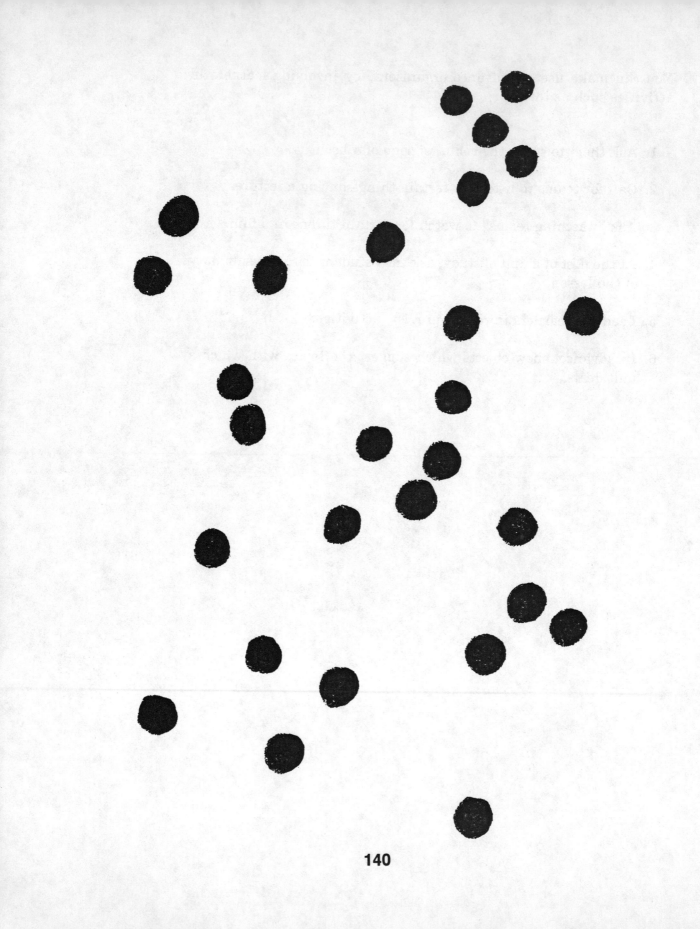

140

● 4. *Provide learners with immediate knowledge of results.*—Teachers use this principle when they call out answers to exams as students grade their own papers. Some learners use flash cards in drill exercises. The back of the card provides knowledge of results.

Learners tend to gain knowledge when they receive immediate knowledge of results. Immediate knowledge of results puts the question and the response (answer) close together. A teacher who provides the student with knowledge of results a week after a test does not use this guideline.

■ **Which of these activities give(s) the learner immediate knowledge of results?**

_____ 1. **A teacher asked, "Who wrote the book of Jeremiah?" A pupil answered, "Jeremiah." The teacher nodded her head in the affirmative.**

_____ 2. **A teacher gave a test of knowledge. Then she said, "Exchange papers and grade." Students graded each other's papers. Then each pupil saw his own test.**

_____ 3. **Both 1 and 2.**

_____ 4. **Neither 1 nor 2.**

In both cases, the pupils received immediate knowledge of results. In number 2 the pupils waited a bit longer to receive knowledge of results. But the short time lapse would make little difference. You should have checked number three.

● Some psychologists prefer to say, "when the learner has immediate confirmation of *correct answers*." This means that the pupil tends to remember facts longer if he receives an immediate reward in the form of knowledge that he answered in the correct way. Knowledge that one made the correct answer serves as a reward in the form of a good feeling about the idea, they say.

■ *Which of the following provide(s) immediate knowledge of results?*

_____ *1. A teacher gave a test. He returned the graded papers two weeks later. He then led a discussion of answers.*

_____ *2. A teacher gave an objective test. While the pupils took the test, he posted the answers on the wall outside the room. As students left, they checked their answers.*

_____ *3. A teacher gave an "open book" test.*

Items two and three give immediate knowledge of results. In number 2, the very short time lapse between the test and checking of results would not detract from the value of the activity. The students still had their minds focused on the questions. In number 3, finding the answers in an "open book" provides immediate knowledge of results. The teacher who postponed returning the papers in number 1 forfeited for the students the values of immediate knowledge of results.

● Use activities such as these to make use of the principle of immediate knowledge of results.

1. Simply nod your head when a student makes a correct response.

2. Give "open book" tests. The learner receives knowledge of results when he finds the answer.

3. Use flash cards for drill purposes. Write questions on one side and answers on the other.

4. When you give a test, post the key outside the door to allow students to check their papers.

5. Return graded papers no later than a day after tests.

6. Use programmed units of study as resources.

● 5. *Involve the learner in numerous and varied activities related to the goal.*—This means the learner should do more than one activity related to a given goal-indicator. This guideline supports the concept that learning means *lasting* change. No two persons achieve learning goals in exactly the same way. One in nine persons has a learning difficulty of some sort. One learner may respond to one kind of activity; another may not. Varied activities will include something for most everyone. The guideline suggests that teachers should confine the learning goals to a few very essential ones. Then they should provide enough activities to produce learning which lasts. Immediate post tests do not really test for lasting change. The teacher should teach as if the pupil's grades depended not upon an immediate post test, but upon a delayed post test given weeks later!

Learners tend to gain knowledge when they take part in numerous and varied activities related to the goal.

The principle which calls for numerous and varied activities suggests also the need for repetition. But the learner should repeat the act in slightly different forms. The chart which follows shows how one may vary learning activities. Note that the activities relate to a given goal. *Each deals with knowing the names of the states.*

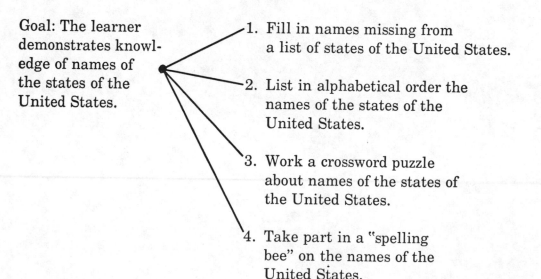

Goal

Goal: The learner demonstrates knowledge of names of the states of the United States.

Activities

1. Fill in names missing from a list of states of the United States.

2. List in alphabetical order the names of the states of the United States.

3. Work a crossword puzzle about names of the states of the United States.

4. Take part in a "spelling bee" on the names of the United States.

Notice that each of the four activities deals with learning the *names of the states,* but in a different way.

144

■ *Would the following activity fit into the four shown above?*

Ask each pupil to draw a map showing the location of the natural resources in the United States.

_____ *Yes*

_____ *No*

The goal-indicator calls for knowledge of names of states. The activity you just read does not deal with names of states. It deals with resources in the United States. The multiple activities must relate to the same goal-indicator. You should have checked no.

■ *Would the following excerpt from a lesson plan reflect use of numerous and varied activities?*

Ask each pupil to assemble a puzzle map consisting of cutouts of the states of Mexico.

_____ *Yes*

_____ *No*

The exercise consists primarily of one activity—working a map puzzle. You should have answered no. One activity does not constitute "numerous and varied" activities!

145

■ *Does the following excerpt reflect the use of numerous and varied activities?*

Ask a team of three pupils to draw on a large piece of cardboard an outline map of Mexico. It should show the names of the various states. Then ask them to cut the map along state lines and make a puzzle map. Ask one pupil to work the puzzle on the floor while the other pupils instruct him. Withdraw several states from the puzzle and ask pupils to name the missing states. Then call out the names of the states. Ask pupils to name the bordering states.

_____ **Yes**

_____ **No**

The plan does call for numerous and varied activities related to the one goal. Each activity focuses on the location of the states of Mexico.

■ *Now, count the activities which the excerpt shown above includes. (The first one says "draw an outline map.") How many do you see?* _____

You should have counted at least five different ones. The verbs in the excerpt give clues: draw, cut, work, name, and so on.

● To make use of the principle of numerous and varied activities, study
first the goal-indicator. Then create several activities related to it.
Verbs like the following will help you think of activities: arrange,
rearrange, write, list, put together, take apart, tell, fill in blanks,
change the form.

● 6. *Involve the learners in novel activities.*—In years gone by, the "spelling bee" and "cyphering match" added novelty to learning. Today students play many other kinds of learning games. They do unusual things. One teacher of writing wanted to impress upon her students the amount of space a newspaper devotes to advertising. The students cut the columns out of a paper and fastened them end to end. Then they stretched the column around the classroom!

Learners tend to gain knowledge when the learning activities involve novel experiences.—When the teacher presents an idea in a novel way, learning tends to endure—unless all the activities involve highly novel experiences. Novelty then loses its appeal.

To show the power of novelty, let's do another experiment. Obtain a watch with a second hand. Then, for only *five seconds* look at page 154. Then return to this page. In the margin of this page list as many of the items as you can remember. Take time now to do it. How many could you list?

Under normal conditions you would have missed several. But you would have remembered the word *power*. Why? It's style and size or print in relation to the other words qualified it as "novel."

■ *Now, look at page 155 for only five seconds. Then list in the margin of this page all the items you can recall. How many did you list? You may have missed some! But you recalled "snake" and "chicken." Why? Novelty took care of that.*

148

■ *Which of these activities make(s) best use of novelty in teaching?*

_____ 1. Show a slide of an organization chart which depicts staff and line relationships among personnel and levels of the organization.

_____ 2. Ask several students to stand at assigned levels on a stairway, in keeping with assigned positions on an organization chart. Ask them to stretch strips of blue paper between them to show staff relationships; red paper to show line relationships.

You must judge. Each uses novelty to some degree. However, most would check item two. A "living organization chart" with real live people in it suggests more novelty than a slide. Both involve other learning principles also, but novelty plays an important role.

● To make use of the principle of novelty, use activities like these.

1. Involve learners in experiments.

2. Ask students to translate ideas into new forms—especially visual forms.

3. Present ideas in cartoon form.

4. Involve learners in making films.

5. Conduct field trips.

CHECK YOUR PROGRESS

■ *You have studied six guidelines for learning which apply especially to gaining knowledge. See how much you can recall about them. Look at the key words at the left. Then in the spaces at the right, restate the guideline.*

Key Word	Explanation
1. active	
2. senses	
3. advance	
4. results	
5. varied	
6. novelty	

Look back at the six parts of this chapter to check your answers.

■ *For review, match the following cases with the principle of learning involved. Most cases involve the use of more than one principle. However, you can probably detect which principle it involves primarily. Not all learning activities will reflect as clearly as these a given principle. Study each case. Ask, What really happens in this case?*

_____ *At the beginning of a unit of study, students looked at a master chart showing the classifications of the books of the Bible.*

_____ *Students looked at flashcards of books of the Bible. Then they turned the cards over to see whether they had classified them properly.*

_____ *The students watched a filmstrip which explained the classification of books of the Bible, and listened to the recorded narration.*

_____ *The students arranged on a full-size bookshelf according to classification a set of book-size blocks. Each block had a book cover showing the name of a book of the Bible.*

_____ *Students took part in all of the activities listed above.*

1. *Involve the learner in activities which call for active response.*

2. *Provide activities in which the learner uses more than one of the senses at the same time.*

3. *Provide activities in which the learner uses advance organizers. (They see in advance the total organization pattern of the information or they establish in advance their intent to learn.)*

4. *Provide for immediate knowledge of results.*

5. *Involve the learner in numerous and varied activities related to the same goal.*

6. *Provide novel activities in regard to the information.*

Check your answers against these: 3, 4, 2, 2 or 6, 5. The principle of active response (number 1) applies to all the cases. That's why we omitted number 1 as an answer. You may argue, and rightly so, that most of them also involve the use of more than one of the senses at the same time and that more than one of them involve the principle of novelty.

As we proceed to the next unit we will study how to recognize learning activities for use in developing understanding. But in doing so, remember that all we have learned about teaching for knowledge helps us to some extent to understand. (Remember the idea of "diffusion of learning" in Unit 1?) But the use of guidelines or principles treated under each heading helps in a special way to bring about learning of the type discussed.

153

ELEMENTS IN A WORSHIP EXPERIENCE

AWARENESS
CONVICTION
CONTRITION
CONFESSION
PETITION
FORGIVENESS
ADORATION
POWER
THANKSGIVING

PIG
DONKEY
MONKEY
PARROT
ARMADILLO
LIZARD
WHALE

PORCUPINE
RABBIT
BUFFALO
RHINOCEROUS
ELEPHANT

UNIT 7

When You Know the Notes to Sing, You Can Sing Most Anything! [1]

(Learning Activities to Help the Pupil Understand)

Why You Will Find the Study Useful:

Most of us want to teach and train so that
   pupils understand as well as know something.

The learning activities you will learn to
   design in this unit will help you teach and
   train for understanding.

Whay You May Expect to Learn:

Goal: A study of this unit should help you
   understand the process of designing learning
   activities for use in teaching and training
   for understanding.

Some Things You Will Do to Prove You Have Achieved This Goal:

* Design learning activities which use the
   guidelines related to teaching and training
   for understanding.
* State the guidelines or principles of learning
   used in given learning activities designed to
   help a pupil understand.

You will need about 2 hours to complete this unit.

---

* Identify the level of understanding which a
  given activity employs.

* Explain the relationship of understanding
  to the six levels of learning.

* List and explain eight of the guidelines or
  principles of learning for use in teaching and
  training for understanding, as used in this unit.

Preview of Terms Used in This Unit:

Understanding.—The five highest levels of learning related to the thought processes. These include comprehension through evaluation. The five do not include the lowest of the six levels—knowledge. (Units 4 and 5 deal with the six levels.)

Translate.—The act of changing a given idea into a new form or recognizing a new form when one sees it.

Interpret.—The act of expanding an idea so as to give further insight as to its meaning.

Transfer.—To use in a new situation something one has learned before.

Problem solving.—The process of finding answers to problems through use of a systematic approach. It involves four to six steps which one follows in a systematic way.

Case study.—An account of a problem situation presented for purposes of analysis. Case studies invite the use of the problem-solving approach to learning.

Probing question.—A question which requires the learner to think deeply and pull together what he knows and understands about many things.

Standard.—Any measure by which one judges something as good.

Units 4 and 5 dealt with the six levels of learning related to knowledge and understanding (cognitive learning). The first level, knowledge, calls for the learner to do such things as recall information. Unit 6 dealt with teaching for knowledge or recall.

This section treats the other five levels. In this study we call these five levels "levels of *understanding*." [1] Thus, evaluation appears as the highest level of understanding. (See chart below.)

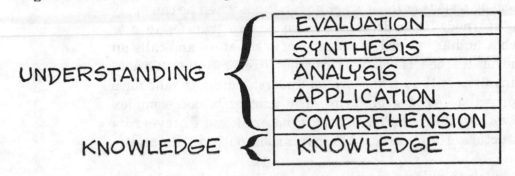

■ *Study the chart carefully. Which of the following indicates the lowest level of understanding?*

_____ *1. Analysis*

_____ *2. Comprehension*

_____ *3. Knowledge*

If you studied the chart carefully, you checked item two—comprehension. You would not have checked "knowledge." Knowledge is not a level of understanding as we use the term here. Knowledge deals mainly with recall of facts. One can know many facts without understanding them. So we place knowledge in a category by itself. Comprehension goes "one step beyond the simple remembering of material," and represents "the lowest level of understanding." [1]

[1] Norman E. Gronlund, *Stating Behavioral Objectives for Classroom Instruction,* New York: The Macmillan Company, 1970, p. 20.

● Let's review the levels of understanding.

Comprehension represents the lowest level of understanding. [2] This means the learner can translate (express ideas in new ways) summarize, and interpret. He can "translate" ideas into new forms. He can interpret the meaning of ideas. He perceives how ideas relate. He has ah-ha moments when he fits facts and ideas together. He sees how one fact relates to another.

Application suggests that the learner understands when he can apply what he has learned. He understands when he can transfer to new situations what he has learned. He faces a new situation and calls up something he has learned. He uses his learning to react to the situation.

Analysis involves still a higher level of understanding. It calls for a planned approach to solving problems. The learner breaks complex material down into its parts. He analyzes material and discovers its form and structure. He finds out its organization pattern. He understands.

Synthesis involves pulling together and relating in the right way things one has learned about a subject. This "pulling together" requires "synthesizing" of many principles and concepts to produce something new. The learner produces a rather complex, creative, and original product. Synthesis calls for understanding at a very high level.

Evaluation calls for making value judgments about processes, ideas, et cetera, according to standards. The learner judges the worth or value of something. He bases his judgment on certain standards.

So we say that comprehension makes up the lowest level of understanding: evaluation the highest. All of these five levels make up what we refer to in this book as *understanding*—one of the four kinds of learning outcomes.

---

[2] *Ibid.*

■ *Which of these statements describe(s) how understanding relates to the six levels learning?*

_____ 1. **All of the six levels of learning constitute levels of understanding.**

_____ 2. **The five highest levels constitute the areas of understanding—comprehension through evaluation. The other level, the lowest of the original six constitutes knowledge.**

You should have checked item two. Remember, the lowest of the six levels (knowledge) represents an outcome in and of itself. The next five levels relate to understanding.

161

● Any activity which helps a learner comprehend, apply, analyze, synthesize, and evaluate develops understanding.

■ **Which of the following best defines** understanding?

_____ 1. *Understanding means the ability to recall facts, information, principles.*

_____ 2. *Understanding means the ability to translate ideas into new and parallel forms.*

_____ 3. *Understanding means the ability to perform at the five highest levels of learning.*

Items one and two do not include as much as three. Number one describes knowledge—not understanding. Number 2 describes only comprehension—the lowest level of understanding. It does not include the higher levels of understanding: application, analysis, synthesis and evaluation. You should have checked number 3.

162

● The eight guidelines or principles of learning dealt with in this unit relate in a special way to all the levels of learning (cognitive) except knowledge. [3] Some of them relate to teaching for comprehension; others to application, analysis, and so on. Many other guidelines apply, but the eight have special value.

To make it easier to "understand" the eight guidelines, we have divided them into two groups of four each.

■ *Study the list below to help you "see in advance" the first four. In a special way they help bring about comprehension and application. Later, this section will present them one at a time. They can serve as a starting point in designing learning activities to bring about understanding.*

1. *Provide learning activities in which the learner changes (translates) ideas into new forms.*

2. *Use activities in which the learner discovers relationships between one idea and another.*

3. *Provide activities in which learners define and interpret ideas and concepts.*

4. *Involve the learner in activities which call for him to use in practical ways what he has learned.*

Now read the guidelines again. Circle in each statement a key word which sets it apart from the others. Do not read further until you have circled the words.

You may have circled words like translates, relationships, define, and use. Other words would do as well as long as they help you recall the principles.

---

[3] Many other principles apply to teaching for understanding. Teachers and leaders should think of these as "starters."

■ *The next exercise asks you to write the guidelines or principles in your own words. You may want to study them further before doing the exercise. Now, using the following key words as "cues," rewrite in your own words the guideline it helps you recall.*

Key Words	Guideline
translate	
relationships	
interpret	
use	

Check your answers with the list of four guidelines shown above.

● Now we will consider the guidelines one at a time. This study should help you recognize learning activities which use the principles.

1. *Use activities in which the learner changes (translates) ideas into new forms.*—Learners tend to understand when they translate or change an idea into a new form; or, when they recognize a new form of an idea. Translation involves at least two kinds of activity: (1) the student himself changes ideas into new forms (translates) or (2) he recognizes new forms (translations) of an idea when he sees them.

Learners tend to develop understanding when they change ideas into new forms.

In the first type of activity, the pupil himself changes something into a new form. He uses his own insights to express an idea in a new way.

■ *Which of these learning activities call(s) for the student to change something into a new form* **himself?**

_____ *1. Ask three students to read aloud John 3:16 from the three translations of the Bible: Moffatt, Williams, and Good News for Modern Man in Today's English Version.*

_____ *2. Ask each pupil to write in his own words (paraphrase) John 3:16.*

In item two the pupil translates on his own. He paraphrases. He expresses an idea in a new form—his own words. In number 1 the pupils simply read translations made by others. You should have checked number two.

165

● A pupil tends to gain understanding when he does the translating himself. But he may also gain understanding when he recognizes a translation which someone else has made. He does not exert as much mental effort as when he makes his own translation. But he does use his mental processes.

For example, a student looks at a translation in the form of a paraphrase. He recognizes that it means the same thing as the original. Or he may look at a drawing or a picture or a chart. He recognizes that it expresses an idea he has read or heard before.

■ *Study the following activity. Does it call for the student to recognize a translation?*

Ask each student to do a clay model which expresses the emotion of anger.

_____ *Yes*

_____ *No*

You should ask yourself, "Does the pupil make the translation himself or does he look at one someone else made? You should have checked no. In this activity the student himself expressed the idea in a new form.

166

■ *Does the following activity call for the student to recognize a translation?*

To conclude the session, ask "Which of the following paraphrases comes closest to the original meaning of Romans 10:9?"

_____ *Yes*

_____ *No*

In this case, the student studies three given paraphrases—done by other persons. He recognizes the correct translation when he sees it. You should have checked yes.

■ *Which of the following learning activities call(s) for recognition of a translation?*

_____ 1. Display the following two charts. Ask, Which of these represents line organization? staff organization?

_____ 2. Distribute to each pupil a set of word strips representing the various departments of organization B. Ask each to arrange the strips on a clingchart so as to picture the line form of organization.

_____ 3. Both 1 and 2.

_____ 4. Neither 1 nor 2.

In item one the pupil looks at two charts. He recognizes the two organization forms. In number 2, he makes his own translation. He arranges the word strips to express the forms of organization. You should have checked number one.

168

■ *Study the following learning activities. Check these which call for the pupil either to change the form of an idea or to recognize a new form (translation).*

_____ 1. *Ask the pupil to draw a simple line drawing which depicts the concept "church."*

_____ 2. *Ask a pupil to read Moffat's translation of 1 Corinthians 13.*

_____ 3. *Ask the pupils to write titles for each of the following three pictures.*

Numbers 1 and 3 call for the pupil to translate into new forms. In number 1, the pupil changes a word, church, into picture form. In number 3, the pupil looks at pictures and changes them into picture titles.

Number 2 involves neither translation nor recognition of a translation. The learner reads a translation someone else has made.

■ *Does the following activity suggest the use of translation? (Remember, pupils may either translate to a new form or recognize a translation.)*

Write on the chalkboard a paraphrase of the Preamble to the Constitution of the United States. Ask the pupils to identify the original source of material.

_____ *1.* Yes

_____ *2.* No

You should have checked yes. The pupils see a translation and recognize it as a restatement of the Preamble to the Constitution. It expresses in parallel form the concepts included in the original Preamble.

● Translations take many forms. First the student may translate written material or spoken material into other words which say the same thing.

■ **Does the student's work shown on the right in the chart below show translation of words into new word forms?**

Original	Student's Work
"I know that my redeemer liveth." (Job 19:25)	I am certain that the one who paid the price for me exists now.

_____ Yes

_____ No

Most would agree that the student's work does express in a new form the same idea as shown In the first. You should have checked yes. Learners also use this principle when they summarize something.

171

● Secondly, learners do the translation themselves when they translate written or spoken material (words) into visual form. Look at any of the cartoons in this book. Note that the meaning expressed in the captions appears in visual form in the drawing.

Thirdly, the learner may reverse the preceding process. He can change a drawing (visual) into words.

■ *Look at the following series of pictures. Make up a title for the series. Write the "title" in the blank.*

TITLE:_____

You have just written a title for the pictures. You may have written "In the Potter's Hand" or "A Workman That Needeth Not to Be Ashamed."

■ *What kind of translation did you do when you wrote the title for the pictures?*

_____ *1. I translated given words into new word forms.*

_____ *2. I translated a visual form into word form.*

_____ *3. I translated a word form into a visual form.*

Of course you should have checked item two. You began with the pictures of a potter at work and ended with a title made up of words.

■ *A teacher led a class in this activity. Study it, then answer the question which follows.*

On the chalkboard I have written the word church. Will each of you do a simple drawing which expresses what "church" means. After you have made the drawing, turn to the student next to you and explain to him your drawing.

The pupils did two translations during the activity. Which of the following describes what they did?

_____ *1. They first translated words into other words, then they translated a drawing into words.*

_____ *2. They first translated a word into visual form: then they translated the visual form into word form.*

_____ *3. They first translated a drawing into words; then they translated words into a drawing.*

You should have checked item two. They translated the word church into a drawing; then they translated the drawing into words as they explained the drawing to the other student.

■ *Now write in your own words the first guideline or principle we have studied.*

1. _____
   _____
   _____

173

● In summary, if you want to make use of the principle that learners tend to understand when they translate (change) ideas into new forms, use activities like these:

(1) Ask the learner to restate an idea *in his own words*.

(2) Ask the learner to summarize something.

(3) Ask the learner to give an example of something.

(4) Ask the learner to change into picture form a written idea.

(5) Ask the learner to change a picture into words.

(6) Ask the learner to change something from one language into another. (English into Spanish, for example.)

(7) Ask the learner to "read" music.

These and many other kinds of activities call for the learner to change the form of something or to recognize a correct translation when he sees it.

● 2. *Use activities in which the learner discovers how one idea relates to other ideas.*—Leaders use this principle when they ask learners to suggest terms associated with given terms. In the act of stating such terms, the learners begin to comprehend. Each associated term defines to some extent the original term. For example, a church school teacher wrote on the chalkboard the word *freedom*. She asked each pupil to suggest other words which came to his mind upon seeing the word. Pupils called out words like liberty, democracy, and dignity. One student comprehended its depth of meaning when he suggested "obligation" and "responsibility." Other students had not thought of the terms. In the process, all the students broadened their understanding of what freedom means.

Another teacher led class members to identify terms related to the word *ethics*. Pupils responded by pointing out such related terms as "rightness" and "relationship." One suggested "oughtness." At that point, class members caught a glimpse of the meaning of ethics.

Learners tend to understand when they discover how one idea relates to other ideas.

■ *Which of the following call(s) for the learner to relate one term to another?*

_____ 1. *A teacher asked the pupils to create an acrostic from the word "love." (An acrostic would consist of four synonyms for love. They would begin with the letters l, o, v, and e.)*

_____ 2. *A teacher asked the pupils to suggest in rapid-fire order the first thing that came to their mind upon hearing the word ecology.*

_____ 3. *Both 1 and 2.*

_____ 4. *Neither 1 nor 2.*

Both call for the student to identify terms related to concepts. In number 1, students associate words with the concept "love." They think of related words which begin with the letters "l," "o," "v," and "e." The activity involves more control over the learning situation than activity number 2. Nevertheless, the pupil identifies and associates terms. Both 1 and 2 suggest a learning activity sometimes referred to as "word association." Much of the value of the method called "word association" rests in this principle. Each associated word serves as an embryo definition which the learner has reasoned out for himself. You should have checked number three.

Use activities in which the learner discovers how one idea
relates to other ideas, associates one idea with another.

■ *Which of the following call(s) for learners to associate one term with another?*

_____ 1. *Ask each student to write a ten-page paper on the meaning of democracy.*

_____ 2. *Ask small study groups to list at least five words they think of when they see the word "democracy." Call for reports. List the terms on the chalkboard. Then ask students to write a word with opposite meaning (antonym) for each of the words.*

_____ 3. *Both 1 and 2.*

_____ 4. *Neither 1 nor 2.*

You should have checked item two. Item two calls for learners to associate one term with others. Even when learners suggest terms with opposite meaning, they use the principle. We call these terms antonyms. For example, "love" becomes clearer in meaning when one places it beside such words as hate. Number 1 helps the learner understand what a term means, but it does not use word association as the approach. It uses a much more complex approach which we will study later.

● Teachers also use the principle when they lead students to discover how one idea or term relates *to another given term.* In order to discover relationships, the learner must have at least two items to think about. In a social studies class a student discovered how "democracy" related to "republic." He listed the similarities and differences between them.

■ *Which of the following excerpts from a lesson plan leads pupils to relate one term to another?*

_____ 1. *Write on the chalkboard a definition of salvation. Ask the pupils to paraphrase the definition and to read it aloud.*

_____ 2. *Ask, which of the following terms expresses more accurately the roles of the church and state in the United States: (1) a wall of separation between church and state; (2) a free church in a free state?*

Item one would tend to lead toward understanding, but it does not teach the pupil to discover relationships. *It involves only one term— salvation. Number 2 involves at least two terms or ideas. The student struggles to discover the relationships. You should have checked number two.*

■ *Does the following activity call for the pupil to discover how one term relates to another given term?*

Ask small study groups to compare the definitions of "salvation" and "conversion," as found in a Bible dictionary. Ask them to list three similarities and three differences between the terms. Call for reports. Then ask the same groups to write a paragraph explaining the differences between the terms.

_____ **Yes**

_____ **No**

It does use the principle. The pupils discover through several activities how conversion relates to salvation.

■ *Now try to write in your own words the first two guidelines or principles this unit has presented up to this point.*

1. _____
   _____

2. _____
   _____

To check you answers refer to the principles on previous pages.

● In summary, if you want to make use of the principle that learners tend to understand when they discover relationships or associate one term with another, use activities like these:

1. Use an activity in which the learner suggests terms he associates with given ideas or concepts (word association method).

2. Ask the learner to suggest words which mean the opposite of given terms (antonyms).

3. Use an activity in which the learner determines how one term relates to another.

4. Lead the learner to compare and contrast ideas in given material, or to list similarities and differences between ideas.

5. Show lists of terms. Ask pupils to pick out terms which belong to the same "family" (for example, apples, oranges, and bananas belong to the family name "fruit"). [3]

_____

[3] Referred to in educational psychology as "generalization."

3. *Use activities in which the learner defines or interprets ideas or concepts.*—One group of students wrote "trial" definitions of "fellowship." Another group compared the definitions of "love" which they found in two word books. Another group looked at a political cartoon and explained what it meant. In each case the pupils defined or interpreted ideas.

Learners tend to understand when they define or interpret ideas or concepts.

■ *Which of these activities call(s) for the student to define or interpret ideas?*

_____ 1. Divide the group into small study groups. Ask each group to work out a statement which explains what "biology" means.

_____ 2. Ask group member to suggest the main teaching of the book of Philippians.

_____ 3. Ask one member to compare the definitions of "redemption" as found in three different dictionaries.

_____ 4. Show the group a copy of a cartoon. Ask them to write in one sentence the idea it conveys.

All four call for the pupils to either define or interpret something. These first three principles apply in a special way when one wants to teach for comprehension.

■ *Now, try to recall and write in your own words the first three guidelines or principles presented thus far in this chapter.*

1. _____

   _____

2. _____

   _____

3. _____

   _____

Check your answers with the statements of principles on page 163 of this unit.

● Use activities such as these to help learners define or interpret ideas or concepts:

1. Ask the learner to study a chart or graph and make interpretations.

2. Ask learners to determine the "central truth" or main idea in a Bible passage.

3. Ask the learner to defend his viewpoint.

4. Show the learner a cartoon (such as a political cartoon). Ask him to tell what it means.

5. Ask learners to write trial definitions of concepts.

6. Lead learners in a "forced word substitution" exercise. Write a passage on the chalkboard. Underline key words. Then ask learners to substitute words or phrases which mean the same thing. Then read the new statement.

A learner interprets when he describes what a cartoon means.

Comprehension happens when you see how one fact relates to another . . .

. . . and have an ah-ha moment

● 4. *Provide activities in which the learner uses (applies) in a new situation what he has learned.*[4]—Students who had learned to read a meterstick, measured the length of a room. They applied what they had learned. A teacher who had learned the principle of using more than one of the senses at the same time, used an audiovisual aid in a class session. Both applied or used in a new situation something they had learned.

To apply means to put into effect or to use in a useful way. The learner transfers his learning. He puts theory into practice. Transfer of learning or application usually means putting to use a single principle or idea rather than a great many at the same time. For example, in mathematics, a pupil learns to compute square root. He transfers (puts into use) his learning when he solves a new square root problem.

Learners tend to understand when they use in a new situation what they have learned.

In the song, "Do-Re-Mi" from Rodgers and Hammerstein's *Sound of Music,* one of the children complains about having to learn the notes of the scale. "But they don't mean anything," she says. Maria answers, "When you know the notes to sing, you can sing most anything!" [5]

Although the illustration involves motor skills, it also illustrates transfer in understanding. The learner masters principles and procedures. He comprehends the concepts involved. Then, he faces a new situation. Can he apply to the new situation what he has learned?

---

[4] Referred to in educational psychology as "transfer of learning."

[5] Rodgers and Hammerstein, *op. cit.*

Application means recalling the facts—and other things you have learned . . .

. and using them in a new situation you haven't faced before!

■ *Which of the following activities calls for the learner to use something he has learned?*

_____ 1. *A pupil who understands the principle of transfer of learning explained it to the other pupils in the class.*

_____ 2. *A pupil understood how to use "advance organizers" in teaching. He then designed an advance organizer to use in teaching the next unit of study for his own class.*

_____ 3. *Both 1 and 2.*

_____ 4. *Neither 1 nor 2.*

Item one has nothing to do with applying learning. The learner simply explains to others. In item two the learner transfers his learning by using the principle in a new situation—the new unit of study. He develops an advance organizer. He goes from learning about advance organizers to using the principle in his own lesson plans. You should have answered number two.

■ *Does the following statement of Jesus call for application of things learned?*

"Why call ye me Lord, Lord, and do not the things I say?" (Luke 6:46).

_____ Yes

_____ No

We believe it does call for the learner to use what he has learned. He transfers learning into real life when he does things based on his learning.

■ *If a learner "transfers" his learning to a new situation, at which of the following levels of learning does he function?*

_____ 1. Knowledge (recall)

_____ 2. Comprehension

_____ 3. Application

Application suggests transfer of learning. You should have checked number three.

CHECK YOUR PROGRESS

● Now, for review of the first four guidelines, label these activities with the guideline each uses. The first one provides an example.

Guideline: *Relate one term to another*

_____ 1. Ask each pupil to explain the difference between verb and adverb.

_____ 2. Ask teaching teams to demonstrate how to use the following learning aids: Flip-chart, filmstrip and poster.

_____ 3. Give pipe cleaners to the pupils. Ask each to design a "piece of art" which suggests the concept of "fellowship."

_____ 4. Write the following words on the chalkboard: cooperation, dependability, integrity. Ask pupils to suggest words which mean the opposite.

_____ 5. Ask learners to write a "trial" definition of "goal."

You probably wrote the guidelines in this order: 1. relate one term to another; 2. use in a new situation what they have learned; 3. translate ideas into new forms; 4. relate one term to another; associate one term with another; 5. define or interpret ideas.

● In summary, if you want to make use of the principle that learners tend to understand when they apply what they learn, use activities like these:

(1) Show a learner how to work a problem, then present him with a set of new ones to work on his own.

(2) Ask the learner to tell how a given situation violates certain rules.

(3) Ask the learner to write a sentence using a given rule of grammar.

(4) Lead teacher-trainees to write learning activities which use a given principle of learning.

(5) Ask the pupil to demonstrate the use of a principle or rule.

(6) Ask the learner to predict what would happen if a person violated a rule.

● You have just completed a study of the first four principles which in a special way apply to teaching for understanding. The first three help at the comprehension level; the fourth at the application level.

Now, let's look at the second group of principles. You will find these helpful in making lesson plans at the higher levels of learning (analysis, synthesis, and evaluation).

To help you see in advance the last four principles for use in teaching for understanding, study the following list. Then we will look more closely at them one at a time.

5. Provide learning activities in which the learners break material down into its parts.

6. Involve learners in activities in which they solve problems in a systematic way.

7. Use learning activities in which the learner combines elements and parts to form a new creative "product."

8. Use learning activities in which the learner judges the value or worth of something, based on given standards.

Look over the list again. Select a key word in each which you feel will help you remember the guideline. *Do not read further until you have selected the words.* Circle them if you wish.

You probably chose such words as parts, systematic, product, and value. Other words would serve as well as long as they help you remember the guidelines.

195

■ *This exercise asks you to write the last four guidelines in your own words. Use the key words suggested. Rewrite the four guidelines.*

Key Words	Guideline
parts	
systematic	
product	
value	

Check your answers with the list which precedes this exercise. You do not have to use the exact wording.

● The following section focuses attention on the last four guidelines one at a time.

5. *Involve the learners in activities in which they break material down into its parts.*—One pupil did a sentence outline of the book of Galatians. Another listened to a piece of music and described its "form." Another listened to a lecture and wrote out the teacher's three main arguments for Federal aid to education. In all three cases the pupils broke material down into its parts.

Learners tend to understand when they break material down into its parts.

■ **Which of these three activities call(s) for the student to break material down into its parts?**

_____ 1. **Ask the students to construct a sentence outline of How to Win Friends and Influence People.**

_____ 2. **Ask the pupils to describe the organization pattern of Peter's sermon in Acts.**

_____ 3. **Ask the pupils to define "lesson plan."**

_____ 4. **Ask students to view a videotape of a teaching session on "The Mediator" and to describe the steps the teacher followed in the teaching plan.**

You should have checked one, three, and four. These three suggest slightly different ways of breaking material down into parts. In number 1 the students outline given material. They discover for themselves the main points and the sub-points. In number 2 the students discover the elements of Peter's sermon based on what they read. The elements become the parts of the sermon. In number 4 the students did not know in advance the planning pattern the teacher followed. By viewing the tapes, they discovered the steps taken.

197

■ *Which of the following activities call(s) for the student to break down material into its parts? Read all four choices before answering.*

_____ 1. *Ask the students to write a paper following a given outline.*

_____ 2. *Ask the students to classify a set of learning activities according to the level of learning each represents.*

_____ 3. *Both 1 and 2.*

_____ 4. *Neither 1 nor 2.*

Neither involves breaking given material down into parts. You should have checked number 4. In number 1 the students receive an outline. Someone else had already broken the material down into its parts. The learner does not do it. In number 2 the learners simply classify a list of things given them.

■ *Now, in your own words, write the fifth guideline (the first in this second group).*

5. _____

_____

Check your answer with the list at the beginning of this section.

● To summarize, provide activities like these to help learners develop understanding by breaking material down into its parts.

1. Ask the learners to outline a given piece of material such as Washington's Farewell Address.

2. Ask the learners to diagram a sentence or a process.

3. Ask them to describe orally or in writing the organization pattern of a given business firm or a church.

● 6. *Involve the learners in activities in which they use a systematic approach to solving problems.*—One group of students faced this problem: How can we best deal with the problem of drugs in XYZ High School? They got the facts, thought them through, and stated ten possible answers. They chose the better ones. They followed the systematic approach to problem solving.

Learners tend to understand when they use a systematic approach to solving problems.

A *problem* is . . .

...AN APPLE HIGHER THAN YOU CAN REACH...

Problem solving involves at least five steps:

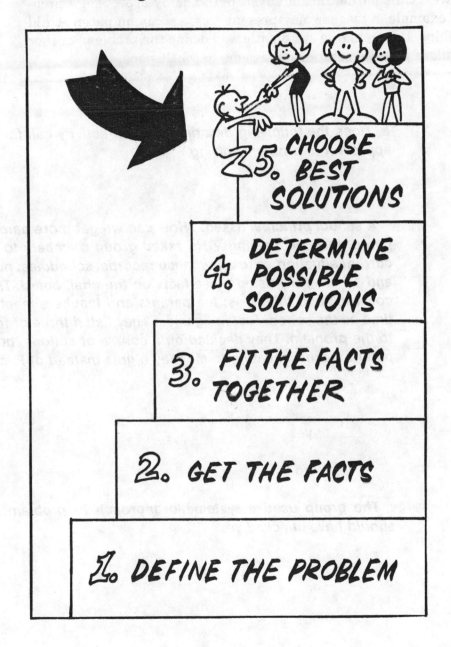

5. CHOOSE BEST SOLUTIONS

4. DETERMINE POSSIBLE SOLUTIONS

3. FIT THE FACTS TOGETHER

2. GET THE FACTS

1. DEFINE THE PROBLEM

● A systematic approach to problem solving usually contains these steps: (1) define the problem; (2) gather the data or facts; (3) fit the facts together to discover relationships; (4) determine possible solutions; (5) select and implement best solutions. This approach, popularized by John Dewey, calls for detailed analysis of the many aspects of a problem. For example, a teacher may present a case study on parent-child relationships. Learners in a systematic way define the problem, gather data, think of possible solutions and come to conclusions.

■ *Does the following description of an activity call for a systematic approach to problem solving?*

A school principal asked, "How can we get more parents to attend parent-teacher meetings? He asked group members to describe the current situation as to attendance records, schedules, publicity used, and so on. They listed these facts on the chalkboard. Then they discovered such things as: the parents and teachers meet at the same time as the school football games! They listed three or four solutions to the problem. They decided on a course of action. They moved the parent-teacher meeting to Monday nights instead of Friday nights.

_____ *yes*

_____ *no*

The group used a systematic approach to problem solving. You should have checked yes.

● To vary the problem-solving approach, the student may analyze an "agree or disagree" statement. For example, a teacher made this statement to a group of teachers in training: "All learning comes through experience. Do you agree or disagree? Why?" In the process learners try to discover the fallacies and truths in a statement. They come to a conclusion.

■ *Does the following activity call for the pupil to analyze whether he agrees or disagrees with a statement?*

To begin the unit, ask the pupils to prove or disprove the statement: "Jeremiah did not write the book of Jeremiah."

_____ *Yes*

_____ *No*

We believe the activity does call for the pupil to agree or disagree. He discovers logical fallacies or truths and thinks in terms of pros and cons. You should have answered yes. The learners search for internal and external data about who wrote the book of Jeremiah.

Problem solving and case studies go together. A case study relates a problem situation for purposes of analysis. We can apply the steps in problem solving when we analyze cases. [6]

---

[6] For a detailed study of problem solving and case studies, see *Using the Case Study in Teaching and Training* and *Using Problem Solving in Teaching and Training* by LeRoy Ford, Broadman Press, Nashville, TN.

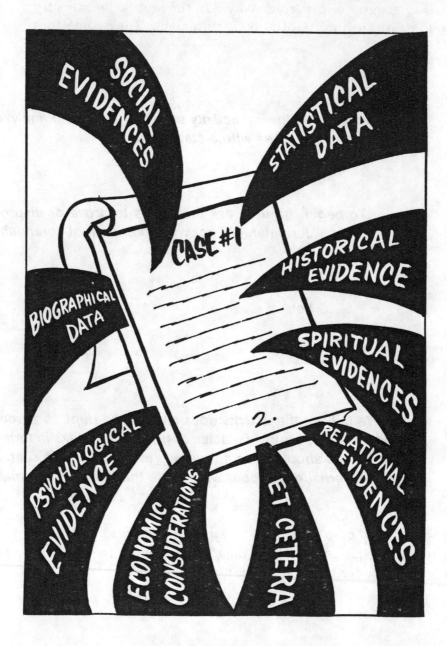

Problem solving and case studies go together.
Cases provide facts to use in problem solving.

■ *In the following list, check the level of learning which "systematic approach to problem solving" and "breaking material down into its parts" represents.*

_____ 6. *Evaluation*

_____ 5. *Synthesis*

_____ 4. *Analysis*

_____ 3. *Application*

_____ 2. *Comprehension*

_____ 1. *Knowledge*

You should have checked analysis, *number four.*

■ *Now, write in your own words the guideline you have just studied. It is guideline number 6 in this unit.*

6. _____
_____

Check your answer with the list of guidelines at the beginning of this section.

● To summarize, use activities like these to involve learners in a systematic approach to problem solving.

1. Brainstorm answers to problems. Pupils suggest in rapid-fire order answers to a problem. Evaluation comes later.

2. Present an hypothesis and ask learners to prove or disprove it.

3. Use creative problem solving. Set before the students an object (such as a piece of sculpture). Ask them to identify it, decide where it came from, and so on. They begin a search. The leader does not give the answers. She only says such things as, "Why do you think it is a _____ ?" Or "Why do you say that?" The learner decides for himself the answer. He supports it with facts he has learned.

4. Make a statement and ask pupils whether they agree or disagree and why.

● 7. *Use learning activities in which the learner puts together elements and parts to form a new "product."*—A teacher asked the students to write a short story on some aspect of life in early America. The students produced a new, creative product—a short story. They had to combine (synthesize) many facts and ideas about early America. They even had to recall and apply what they knew about English composition and techniques of short story writing. A teacher asked the pupils to work out a new system for keeping subject files up to date. They produced a new product—a filing system. It required that they put together what they knew and understood about filing. A social studies teacher asked this probing question: Describe the role of the Monroe Doctrine in affairs between countries. The pupil had to draw from all he understood about the many parts of the subject. He put them together to form his own rather complex answer. It showed his own creative viewpoint.

Learners tend to understand when they put elements and parts together to form a whole—a new product.

● Asking *probing* questions calls for students to put together the parts of something. They produce a product—a new, creative answer. Some questions call for thought at the comprehension level. Others require response at the application level, others at the analysis level, and so on. [7] Probing, thought-provoking questions—unusual questions—call for the learner to reflect on all he knows and understands about the problem. He "synthesizes" an answer to a complex question.

■ *In your opinion, which of the following would you call "probing questions"?*

_____ 1. *According to the Baptist Faith and Message, what does sin mean?*

_____ 2. *If God has forgiven all our sin, does that mean he has already forgiven us the sins we will commit next week? Explain.*

_____ 3. *What would happen if God should suddenly withdraw his grace from us?*

We asked for what you thought. We checked items two, three. Number 1 does not probe a great deal. It simply calls for the person to recall or perhaps to express in his own words what a statement says.

_____

[7] For a comprehensive treatment of how to ask questions to call for responses at the various levels of learning, see *Classroom Questions: What Kinds?* Norris N. Sanders (New York: Harper and Row, 1966).

Asking probing questions calls for the learner to put
elements and parts together—to form a new, creative answer!

■ *Which of the following questions probe(s) the learners' thoughts?* *Read all four alternatives.*

_____ 1. *"Whom say ye that I am?" (Luke 9:20).*

_____ 2. *"Shall we continue in sin, that grace may abound?" (Rom. 6:1).*

_____ 3. *Both 1 and 2.*

_____ 4. *Neither 1 nor 2.*

We would check one and two. They cause the learner to think deeply in order to answer. The answer would reflect the learner's thoughts on many facets of the question.

■ *Into which of the following levels of learning would answering a probing question fit?*

_____ *Evaluation*

_____ *Synthesis*

_____ *Analysis*

_____ *Application*

_____ *Comprehension*

The writer feels that answering a probing question would fall within the level of synthesis. For example, the question, What could happen if God should withdraw his grace from us? calls for the learner to create an answer. He puts together many bits of insight. He would have to "synthesize," put together what he understands about the doctrines of God, sin, grace, and so on.

212

● Learners use this guideline when they work out complex projects which require them to use and apply *many* principles and concepts. They make practical use of what they have learned, but on a larger scale than when they simply apply a given principle to a new situation. When they use many principles to form a new product, we call this "synthesis." The learner "synthesizes" a great many things he has learned in order to do a more complex project.

For example, a trainee learns all of the principles for writing a term paper. He learns how to organize ideas. He learns how to explain and record data. He learns to summarize, and so on. Then he writes an original term paper. To do so he synthesizes or pulls together and uses many principles related to preparing research papers.

■ *Which of the following activities would represent "synthesis" of many parts into a new whole? (Note the four alternatives.)*

_____ 1. *A teacher-trainee writes a complete lesson plan on "The Effects of the Industrial Revolution on the Growth of American Cities."*

_____ 2. *The learner writes an original feature article for a magazine.*

_____ 3. *Both 1 and 2.*

_____ 4. *Neither 1 nor 2.*

One and two call for the use of many principles. In each, the learner uses in a meaningful way many of the things he has learned about the subject. He produces a new product. The lesson plan requires the use of what the trainee has learned about writing goals and indicators, choosing activities, and so on. He puts all of this into a new product—a new lesson plan. In number 2 the learner has learned many pointers about writing: how to get attention, what kind of format to use, and so on. He pulls them all together and writes an original feature article. It reflects his understanding of many things about journalism. You should have checked number three.

■ *If a learner (1) builds a new lesson plan or (2) writes an original feature article, at which level of learning does he function?*

_____ *Knowledge*

_____ *Comprehension*

_____ *Application*

_____ *Analysis*

_____ *Synthesis*

_____ *Evaluation*

The learner "synthesizes" in both cases. You should have checked "synthesis." But remember, when a learner functions at a given level, he at the same time functions to some extent at all the preceding levels. In both cases, the learner recalls (knowledge), comprehends, and applies individual principles (transfers). He probably analyzes the subject before trying to write the lesson plan and the article. But finally his product calls for synthesis. Doing things at any given level requires ability to function at all the preceding levels.

■ *Now, write in your own words guideline 7.*

7. _____
   _____

Check your answer with the list in the first part of this section.

● Use activities like these to help learners put together parts and elements to form a new creative "product."

1. Ask a probing question.

2. Ask the learner to write a play, a poem, or a story.

3. Ask the learner to develop a new plan for doing something (like taking a census).

4. Assign a research paper (like "How Climate Affects Agriculture").

5. Call on the learner to compose a new piece of music.

● 8. *Use learning activities in which the learner judges value or worth of something, based on given standards.*—A teacher asked a pupil to judge (evaluate) a hymn on the basis of whether it reflected the doctrines of a given church. Another asked a group of teacher-trainees to select the right furniture for a preschool room. Another asked the pupils to rank automobiles according to safety factors needed for mountain driving. In all cases they judged value on the basis of given standards.

Learners tend to understand when they judge the value of something, based on given standards.

Evaluation assumes the existence of something to be evaluated. For example, a learner may look at three approaches to arranging a classroom. He determines the needs of the course and the nature of the pupils. Then he states some standards by which he judges the arrangement. In the light of these standards, he chooses one of the three. He ranks the approaches in order of value.

■ *Which of the following activities call(s) for the learner to judge the worth of something? (Remember to ask, "Does the activity call for the learner to judge value based on either stated or implied standards?")*

_____ 1. *In a public speaking contest, a panel of student judges chose from three speakers the one to speak at the district meet.*

_____ 2. *A group of students in a curriculum design class studied the periodicals in a certain series. They determined the characteristics of the series.*

_____ 3. *A group of students in a curriculum design class studied a case description of a church. Then they made a "recommendation" as to which curriculum series the church should use.*

In one and three the students make judgments as to the relative value of several givens. In number 1 they rank the speakers according to certain standards of a good speech. In number 3 they rank several curriculum series as to their value in meeting the needs of a given church. Decisions as to the degree to which something meets standards involves evaluation. Number 2 simply calls for analysis of some given material.

■ *Does the following activity call for learning at the evaluation level?*

Ask the students to rank the three designs according to their relatives merit in (1) layout and (2) use of color.

_____ *Yes*

_____ *No*

The pupils judges the designs on the basis of good layout and use of color. You should have checked yes.

217

CHECK YOUR PROGRESS

● Now, use the key words shown below to write in your own words the second group of four guidelines to use in teaching for understanding.

Key Word   Guideline

Key Word	Guideline
parts	
systematic	
new product	
evaluate/judge	

Check your answers with those at the beginning of this section.

218

● To review how these guidelines relate to learning activities, match the following activities with the guideline or principle each seems to use.

Activities

_____ 1. Ask class members to choose the furniture suitable for a doctor's waiting room.

1. translate into new forms

_____ 2. Lead the class to analyze this question: How can we increase sales of school newspapers?

2. judge the value or worth based on standards.

_____ 3. Ask each work group to write an original fifteen-minute one-act play.

3. discover how one idea relates to another

_____ 4. Ask each member to outline chapter 1 in *The Power of the Listening Ear.*

4. break down into parts

_____ 5. Ask members to do a simple drawing which conveys what "conflict" means.

5. put parts together to form a new, creative product

_____ 6. Call on the pupils to suggest words which come to mind when they see the word *peace.*

6. use a systematic approach to problem solving

You probably answered in this order: 2, 6, 5, 4, 1, and 3.

● Teachers may decide that a session calls for the primary learning outcome of understanding. They can use these eight guidelines (and many others) to design the right kinds of learning activities to use in teaching. This list of eight by no means contains all of the possible guidelines. However, mastery of those should give the teacher much help in designing learning activities which relate to development of understanding.

219

● In summary, use activities such as these to lead learners to judge the worth or value of things:

1. Ask them to rank several items in order of value according to certain standards.

2. Present a case study—in story form or in a picture form. Ask students to point out the fallacies in what the case portrays. For example, they may study a picture of a person making a hospital visit and determine what the visitor did wrong. (Implies a set of standards for hospital visitation.)

3. Determine whether a novel meets the standards of a good novel.

4. Rate a piece of art according to standard of excellence.

**ATTITUDES
AND
VALUES
OUTCOMES**

UNIT 8

Try It! Try It! You'll Like It!—Like It! Like It! You'll Try It!
(Learning Activities for Teaching Attitudes and Values)

Why You Will Find the Study Useful:

The learning activities you will learn to design
in this unit will help you do a better job of
a difficult task—teaching and training for
change in attitude.

Why You May Expect to Learn:

Goal: A study of this unit should help you understand the process of designing learning activities
for use in teaching and training for change in
attitudes and values.

Some Things You Will Do to Prove You Have Achieved This Goal:

* Design learning activities which use the
principles of learning (or guidelines) related
to development of attitudes and values.

* State the guidelines or principles of learning
used in a given learning activity.

* Recall and explain the nine guidelines for use
in developing attitudes and values, as shown in
this unit. [1]

You will need about 1 hour and 30 minutes to complete this unit.

---

[1] This unit presents only nine of the many guidelines of principles of learning which
in a special way relate to attitudes and values as a learning outcome. The principles do
not apply solely to attitudes and values as an outcome. They also prove effective in
teaching and training for other outcomes.

Preview of Terms Used in This Unit:

Attitude.—A mind-set or viewpoint toward a person, place, or idea.

Climate of Freedom.—A group "atmosphere" in which each member senses acceptance of himself by others and feels free to express his own feelings.

Emotional experience.—An experience which deeply affects a person's feelings toward an object or idea.

Positive action.—An action taken as a result of a willful decision to do a thing.

Value.—The relative worth of a thing in light of a person's assessment of it. Closely related to attitudes.

UNIT 8

"Try It! Try It! You'll Like It!—Like It! Like It! You'll Try It!"
(Learning Activities for Teaching Attitudes and Values)

"Attitudes," so one educator said, "develop as desirable by-products" of other learning outcomes (knowledge, understanding, skills.) In this sense, teaching and training for change in knowledge, understanding, and skill help bring about change in attitudes and values.

Attitudes reflect mind-sets toward persons, places, things and ideas. Teaching for change in attitude requires the leader to accept less concrete indicators of learning than for the other kinds of learning. Teachers find it more difficult to plan for change in attitude than for other kinds of change. "A man convinced against his will, is of the same opinion still." Adamant mind-sets toward persons, places, things, and ideas seem to defy change. Many teachers simply prefer to ignore the need for teaching of attitudes and values. Others seek to learn what psychology has to offer. They do their best to apply the principles in the design of learning activities.

But attitudes *can* change. Values can change. A man previously blind said to Jesus, "Whereas I was blind, now I see" (John 9:25). He meant not only physical blindness but attitudinal blindness. How do attitudes and values change? When attitudes do change, what conditions seem to have produced the change?

As in all the learning outcomes a great many guidelines and principles of learning relate to changing attitudes and values. When applied, they tend to lead toward change. They do not guarantee change. Too many factors come into play to make this possible. The wise teacher studies the guidelines which affect attitude change. He applies them as best as he knows how. Then he waits with patience for things to happen to show that change has occurred.

This unit treats nine guidelines for use in teaching for change in attitudes and values. To help you understand the nine guidelines, we have divided them into two groups. The first group includes four; the second, five.

Study the list below to help you "see in advance" the first four guidelines. In a special way they help us in teaching for change in attitudes and values. Later this unit will present them one at a time.

1. Arrange for learners to observe leaders and peers who set the right example; who exemplify the attitude.

2. Arrange for learners to read or hear about persons who exemplify the attitude.

3. Arrange for learners to confront sources which they consider authoritative.

4. Help the learners identify and specify the attitude and learn what the attitude means.

■ *Read the guidelines (principles) again. Circle in each statement a key word which sets it apart from the others.* **Do not read further until you have circled the words.**

Words like these stand out: example, read-hear, authoritative, and identify. You may have circled others.

■ *The exercise below asks you to write the guidelines in your own words. You may use the key words at the left as clues.*

Key Words	Guideline
example	
read-hear	
authoritative	
identify	

Check your work with the list above. You need not use the exact words.

■ *Now, in the space below, try to recall and write the first four guidelines this unit suggests for teaching for change in attitudes and values.*

1. _____
   _____

2. _____
   _____

3. _____
   _____

4. _____
   _____

Check your answers with the list at the beginning of the chapter.

● By way of review, review the following process for determining the right kind of learning activities:

The learning goal tells us the primary learning outcome (knowledge, understanding, skill, attitude). The primary outcome gives us clues to which guidelines to use to design the right kind of learning activities. The learner uses the activities to achieve the goal. (See Unit 3.)

● Study the first four guidelines or principles of learning which when applied, tend to result in change in attitude and values.

1. *Arrange for learners to observe persons who set the right example; who exemplify the attitude.*—Many of the greatest teachers have never taught in a classroom. They never speak in public. They simply move among people—*being* the right kind of person. They reflect the right kinds of values and ideals.

■ **Which of the following statements reflect the spirit of this guideline?**

_____ 1. **A public school teacher said, "What I do after the bell rings is my own business."**

_____ 2. **A church school teacher, preparing an attitudinal lesson said, "For all practical purposes I have already taught that lesson."**

_____ 3. **One person defined "true teacher" as "one whose very presence causes learning to take place."**

You perhaps checked two and three. In one the alert public-school teacher knows that what he does after school does in fact become the pupil's business! "You are not your own; you are bought with a price." Attitudes affect ideals and life-styles.

THE LEADER EXEMPLIFIES THE ATTITUDE!

"BE YE KIND" LIKE THE BIBLE SAYS OR I'LL HIT YOU OVER THE HEAD!

I'M COPYING THE SECTION ON CHRISTIAN ETHICS SO MY STUDENTS DON'T HAVE TO BUY THE BOOK!

© 1976. Adapted from John V. Lawling, Jr. Used by permission.

Inconsistency in a teacher-trainer's life teaches inconsistency. A teacher who tries to teach love instead of hate, and compassion instead of unconcern, had better look at his *own* record. The potential for changing pupil attitudes looms high. The teacher of youth should know that by nature youth seek heroes after whom they can model their lives. The teacher's own life-style must reflect the attitudes he teaches.

This principle says to parents, "Know your children's friends." Friends influence friends.

Learners tend to change attitudes when they observe leaders or peers who set the example; who exemplify the attitude.

● One finds it difficult to design "activities" which use the principle of personal example. Such learning activities belong in a class by themselves. We find it hard to express them in terms of things to do in the classroom. The pupil finds himself doing activities like these: (1) watching the actions of a person who sets an example; (2) listening to personal testimonies; (3) noting the degree of integrity or sham which he sees; (4) shaping his own actions in the light of what he sees. Jesus "went about doing good." The teacher can best use the principle by following Jesus' example.

■ *Which of the following learning activities employ(s) this guideline?*

_____ 1. *Ask the learner to write a trial definition of "respect."*

_____ 2. *Invite to the session a worker with children who cannot hear. Ask him to tell about some of the rewards of his work.*

_____ 3. *Both 1 and 2.*

_____ 4. *Neither 1 nor 2.*

You should have checked item two. The learner meets firsthand a person who exemplifies concern for children who cannot hear. In number 1, the learners simply try to find out what "respect" means.

233

● In summary, to make use of the guideline related to personal example, use activities like these:

1. Let the pupils observe *your own* life!

2. Invite others who exemplify the attitude to work with the pupils.

3. Take field trips where students meet persons who exemplify the attitude.

4. Arrange activities in which students work or play with others in their own age group who "model" the attitude.

2. *Arrange for learners to read or hear about others who exemplify the attitude.*—Some teachers make it a habit to ask pupils to read great biographies. Others provide audio tapes of material done by people who set the example. The learners read or hear—or in some other way learn *vicariously* about persons who model the attitude.

Closely related to the guideline concerned with personal example, this guideline suggests other learning activities. Reading and hearing about others who model an attitude serve as the next best thing to knowing personally an "exemplifier" of attitude. Jesus used parables to depict both positive and negative example setters. Consider the parables of the good Samaritan and the prodigal son as examples.

■ *Which of the these activities would call for the student to read or hear about a person who models the attitude (as opposed to having direct contact with the person)?*

_____ 1. **Ask one student to present a five-minute review of a biography of Abraham Lincoln. Suggest that he point out incidents which show "love of country."**

_____ 2. **Ask students in small groups of four to tell each other an experience in which they could have acted dishonestly but instead, chose to make an honest response.**

_____ 3. **Both 1 and 2.**

_____ 4. **Neither 1 nor 2.**

Item one uses the example of others; item two uses personal example. *You should have checked number one.*

Learners tend to change attitudes when they read or hear about persons who exemplify the attitude.

● In summary, use activities such as these to help learners read or hear about persons who set the example:

1. Assign or suggest biographies for reading.

2. Play audio or video tapes about persons who serve as examples.

3. Present motion pictures of lives of persons who set the example.

4. Enlist pupils to act in dramas which deal with persons who set the example.

5. Read letters from persons who set the example.

3. *Expose learners to authoritative sources.*—Students use this guideline when they study statistical reports and books by authors with wide experience in a field.

Learners tend to experience some change in attitude when they confront sources which they consider authoritative. The words "which they consider" provide a key to the change. Many times learners think, "If he said it, it must be true." Because they accept the person, they tend to accept his advice. This guideline reflects also the power of personal example.

The guideline or principle tends to have more effect when the learner sees the authority in person. Expressions on the face and tones of voice help convince the learner.

Reports of research may also serve as "authoritative" sources. The source does not have to consist of persons. For example, a report of a church budget could cause a church member to decide he ought to tithe.

Learners tend to change attitudes somewhat when they confront sources which they consider authoritative.

■ **Which of these activities expose(s) the learner to authoritative sources?**

_____ 1. Ask a panel of three housewives to discuss among themselves before the group the dangers of exposure to radiation.

_____ 2. Invite to the session a medical doctor to speak for fifteen minutes on the topic "Radiation and Cancer."

_____ 3. Both 1 and 2.

_____ 4. Neither 1 nor 2.

Item two applies the principle. Unless the housewives in item one know the subject, they could better discuss how to make children obey at home.

● Teachers and leaders may use such activities as these to expose learners to authoritative sources.

1. Involve them in study of the authoritative source—the Bible.

2. Arrange for them to see and hear persons who speak with authority in their field.

3. Ask them to read authoritative books.

4. Involve them in study of research reports.

5. Ask them to interview authorities and report.

4. *Help the learners identify and specify attitudes and learn what the attitudes mean.*—Learners use this guideline when they read a Scripture passage (such as the story of the good Samaritan) and pinpoint the attitudes involved (compassion, for example). They use it when they describe their own feelings toward persons, places and things.

Learners tend to experience some change in attitude when they identify and specify the attitude; when they learn what the attitude means.

The learner who knows the kind of change he should make stands a better chance of making the change. To identify an attitude means to study the context of a problem and to decide which attitude lies at center. Most people find it hard to identify attitudes. Simply making a list of attitudes requires more thought than one might expect. Listing negative attitudes, then stating the positive aspect of each sometimes helps one to pinpoint attitudes.

■ *Which of these activities call(s) for the learner to identify an attitude?*

_____ *1. From a list of attitudes which seem related to the study, ask pupils to choose the one which seems to express best the attitude involved.*

_____ *2. Ask a successful parent to present to the group a fifteen-minute talk on discipline in the home.*

_____ *3. Both 1 and 2.*

_____ *4. Neither 1 nor 2.*

Item one calls for use of the guideline. The pupils identify and pinpoint an attitude. Number 2 suggests a valid thing to do but it uses the principle of personal example.

● After the students identify an attitude, they need to learn what it means. Many assume that they know what an attitude means. But when they try to express it, they hesitate. For example, what does "compassion" or "respect for other persons" really mean? Finding out the meaning of an attitude opens up new points of view toward persons, places, things, and ideas.

■ *Which of these learning activities help(s) learners find out what an attitude means?*

_____ 1. *Ask three pupils to read aloud from three dictionaries (including a Bible dictionary) the meaning of the word "love." Ask them to list ways the definitions differ.*

_____ 2. *Begin the session by asking pupils to write a trial definition of the term "respect."*

_____ 3. *Ask members to do a simple line drawing which shows what respect for one's fellowman means. Ask them to explain their drawings to each other.*

All of these call for the learner to define an attitude. The approaches differ.

240

● Activities like these help the learner identify and define attitudes:

1. From a list of attitudes select those which a given story illustrates.

2. Make up stories which illustrate an attitude.

3. Write trial definitions of given attitudes. Compare the statements with what a dictionary says.

4. In a given story, circle phrases which suggest an attitude.

5. Write words which mean the same and words which mean the opposite of given attitudes.

● The second group of guidelines related to teaching for change in attitudes and values appears below. We start numbering with number 5 since you have already studied the first four.

5. Provide ways for learners to have meaningful emotional experiences.

6. Arrange for learners to take positive action in regard to the attitude; to practice the attitude in situations which call for it.

7. Provide opportunities for learners to analyze their own values; to practice making decisions on moral and ethical issues.

8. Provide activities in which learners reflect upon their own life experiences in the light of eternal truth.

9. Arrange for learners to share their insights with others in a climate of freedom.

To help you recall the guidelines circle in these five a key word. *Do not read further until you select and circle the words.*

You may have chosen these key words: emotional, positive action, decisions, reflect, and share. Other words will serve as well as long as they help you recall.

■ *Without looking at the list above, try to write in your own words the last group of five guidelines. A key word appears at the left to serve as a clue.*

Key Word	Guideline
emotional	
positive action	
decisions	
reflect	
share	

Check your answers with the list on the previous page.

243

5. *Provide ways for learners to have meaningful emotional experiences.*—One teacher read dramatically the account of the crucifixion. Another took a group of students to visit patients in a home for the aging. Another teacher asked pupils to read *Angel Unaware*. [1] All three cases had emotional appeal.

Learners tend to experience some change in attitude when they face meaningful emotional experiences.

What becomes a meaningful emotional experience for one person may not do so for someone else. In the final analysis, a teacher can only invite persons to learn. Sometimes going on a trip or reading a well-written essay stirs the emotions. Throughout history, impassioned speeches have brought about emotional responses. Sometimes essays or poems on subjects of an emotional nature tend to implement the principle. Viewing motion pictures and reading novels can create the conditions which appeal to the emotions.

■ *Which of these activities would employ the principle of emotional appeal?*

_____ 1. *Give each person a sheet of plain paper. Ask group members to imagine that the paper represents the person they hold most dear in life. They should recall the person's name and the reasons they consider him dear. Then ask them to crumple the paper in their hands. Then ask them to try to put the paper back into its original condition. Ask those who could not crumple the paper to explain why.*

_____ 2. *Display a picture of a child standing in the midst of the rubble of war. Ask members to compose a "thought narration" of the child's feelings and to share it with the group.*

_____ 3. *Ask each member to write an original essay of not more than 300 words on the subject: "If I Had Only Twenty-four Hours to Live."*

Each of the activities in a different way could produce an emotional response. Number 1 calls for the transfer of emotion to an inanimate object. Numbers 2 and 3 use the person's capacity to reflect, imagine, and project, to create an emotional response.

---

[1] By Dale Evans Rogers.

244

● In summary, you can lead the learner to have emotional experiences with meaning by using such activities as these:

1. Display flat pictures which have emotional appeal.

2. Ask pupils to explain feelings shown in flat pictures.

3. Read newspaper articles which appeal to the emotions.

4. Present motion pictures which appeal to the emotions.

5. Ask pupils to read books which have emotional appeal.

6. Ask pupils to write essays on subjects which involve the emotions.

7. Take field trips for firsthand contact with real life.

8. Involve pupils in the use of drama.

9. Read dramatically a story or essay.

6. *Lead learners to take positive action.*—Jesus said, "Do good to them that hate you" (Matt. 5:44). A learner who felt deeply hostile toward his supervisor came to his teacher for advice. The learner later volunteered to sit at the hospital with the child of the supervisor. He took positive action in regard to his attitude.

Learners tend to experience some change in attitude when they take positive action in regard to the attitude; when they exercise (practice) the attitude in situations which call for it.

This principle suggests that if a learner by an act of will takes positive action, his attitude tends to change. If a person hates someone or something, his attitude may change if he, by an act of will deliberately does specific things (takes action) to express love. "Your own soul is nourished when you are kind" (Prov. 11:17, TLB). The learner does not just "think" about this action or make promises about what he should do. He takes the action.

■ *Does the following statement reflect the power of positive action?*

It is easier to act your way into a new way of feeling than to feel your way into a new way of acting.

_____ Yes

_____ No

We believe that it does reflect the power of positive action in changing attitudes. This does not negate the idea of feeling coming first. The traffic on "Action-Feeling" street moves in both directions. Teachers may provide real or made-up situations which call for the learner to practice an attitude. The use of role playing thrusts learners into made up situations where they "practice" attitudes.

246

■ Contact with the real world calls for learners to adjust and react. For example, trips to children's homes cause the learner to face up to his attitudes and change them if necessary.

Which of these activities call(s) for the learner to take positive action?

_____ 1. On the chalkboard write the following attitudes: contentment, peace, respect, love, compassion, acceptance. Ask group members to state a word which means the opposite. Write the words beside the original list.

_____ 2. In advance, ask a team of four members to make a survey of physical needs of at least ten families in the downtown area of your city. Ask them to report their findings at the beginning of the unit.

_____ 3. Ask a team of two boys to visit the men's "tank" at a county or city jail. Ask them to keep in mind during the visit these questions: . . . Call for a report on what the group can do to meet the needs of the persons.

We believe that numbers 2 and 3 call for use of the principle. They involve learners in real life situations. Number 1 simply calls for learning what given attitudes mean.

● The objectives (indicators) in the goal-indicator statement give clues to possible positive actions. If one teaches for change in attitude, he can often use the *indicators* as positive action activities. For example, look carefully at the following breakdown of a goal-indicator related to attitude.

The student will demonstrate an attitude of concern for the physical needs of political refugees   →   by doing such things as   →

1. Distributing basic food items.

2. Investigating services which agencies can provide.

3. Assisting with cooking responsibilities.

4. Volunteering to make collections of money.

The list of indicators could just as well fall under the caption "possible positive actions." By taking part in the activities (listed as indicators), learners use many of the learning principles used in teaching for change of attitude. Thus, in the example shown, a teacher could use as a learning activity the distribution of food items. Learners *practice* the attitude. They have meaningful emotional experiences. But many activities like these can take place only *outside* the classroom! So what? If attitude change requires this type of activity, then the teacher should make plans for using them.

248

● Try using activities like these to involve learners in positive action:

1. Assign learners to visit prospects and report back.

2. Lead learners to establish a "clothing closet" at the church.

3. Arrange for learners to do volunteer work at a school for retarded children.

4. Suggest that learners do something good for a person whom they feel may have wronged them. Ask for reports.

5. Take a field trip to a children's home or a home for the aging.

6. Take a field trip to a school or church where persons speak Spanish—or some other language.

7. Arrange for learners to survey needs among people near them.

8. Write letters to members of Congress urging them to vote for or against a bill.

7. *Provide opportunities for learners to analyze their own values; to practice making decisions on moral and ethical problems.*—A teacher read a case study which involved the problem of cheating. She ended it by asking, "What would you do?" Learners practiced making decisions. Another involved the learners in playing "The Game of Democracy." The learners played the role of members of Congress. They had to choose whether to vote for or against a bill which would compromise their convictions.

Learners tend to experience some change in attitude when they analyze their own values; when they practice making decisions on moral and ethical problems.

■ **Look at the cartoon on the next page. Does it provide practice in making decisions?**

_____ **Yes**

_____ **No**

A pupil who filled in the answer in the cartoon would practice making a decision.

■ *Any activity which causes the learner to think about his own value system uses this guideline. Many persons seldom reflect on their own sense of values. Both parents and teachers can lead learners to think about their value system.*

Would the following activity cause a learner to analyze in some way his values?

Ask the learner to draw a picture of the kind of house he would like to live in or the kind of neighborhood he would like to play in.

_____ *Yes*

_____ *No*

The learner would tend to express his values in the picture. The teacher can cause the learner to think further by asking questions like, What do you want most in the house? Do you feel it is really important to have it?

GETTING OUR VALUES STRAIGHT! "HOW LONG HALT YE BETWEEN TWO OPINIONS?"

■ *Would this activity cause the learner to analyze his value system?*

Ask the learners to study this case, then check an answer: A boy found a brand-new football he knows another youngster has stolen. Which of these actions should the boy take?

_____ *return the football to the storekeeper*

_____ *give it back to the thief*

_____ *keep it himself*

_____ *leave it where he found it*

_____ *other:* _____

■ *Do you believe the activity causes the learner to analyze his values?*

_____ *Yes*

_____ *No*

The answers the learner gives really tell what the learner feels he himself should do in the case. We believe you should have answered yes.

● Use activities like these to guide the learner in making decisions on moral (and ethical) problems; analyzing own value.

1. Use cartoon cases in which the learner writes in his decision. (See cartoon, pages 256-57.)

2. Ask learners to role-play situations in which they must make decisions between right and wrong.

3. Present a case study, then ask, What would *you* do?

4. Use "games" which call for the learner to make moral and ethical decisions.

5. Present a case study, then ask learners which of three or four given actions they ought to take.

6. Ask learners to draw pictures of things they would like to be, do, or possess. Ask them to explain.

7. Ask learners to analyze TV commercials. Ask questions like, To what value did the commercial appeal? Did it appeal to something which you believe important? Did it exploit the viewer?

8. Allow pupils to help decide on rules for classroom or family living.

MR. HAMMOND: NEVER MARRIED; POLITICALLY LIBERAL; MEMBER TWO CIVIC SERVICE CLUBS; OWNS A CHAIN OF DRIVE-IN RESTAURANTS; GREW UP IN MIDDLE-CLASS FARM FAMILY; SIXTY YEARS OF AGE; ATTENDS CHURCH IRREGULARLY BUT HAS NEVER BEEN A MEMBER

MRS. GRANVIL: HAS NO CHILDREN; WIDOW; GREW UP IN UPPER-CLASS FAMILY; SPENDS WINTERS IN SUMMER HOME; SPONSORS AN INTERNATIONAL ART FESTIVAL; VOTES A CONSERVATIVE TICKET; FORTY-NINE YEARS OF AGE

MR. GRAYSON: GREW UP IN POVERTY; COMPLETED PH.D. IN ECONOMICS; HAS TWO TEEN-AGE SONS OF HIS OWN; SPONSORS A ROYAL AMBASSADORS' SOFTBALL TEAM; DOES VOLUNTEER SOCIAL WORK WITH A MISSION ACTION GROUP; THIRTY-FIVE YEARS OF AGE

One can analyze his own values—through the eyes of others. How would each of these people tend to react to the problem?

. . . tend to react to this problem?

● 8. *Provide ways for learners to reflect upon their life experiences in the light of truth.*—Teachers use this guideline when they ask such questions as: (1) Tell of an act which another person did in your behalf, and express how you felt toward that person. (2) Who in your life has meant more to you than any other person. Why? (3) In the light of Paul's teaching in 1 Corinthians 13 what changes do you feel you should make in your life? Teachers use this guideline when they ask learners to explain why they do or do not identify with characters in a novel. Jesus used the principle when he said to Peter, "Lovest thou me?"

To reflect means to ponder some subject matter, idea, or purpose with a view to understanding it in the light of truth. It means thinking about the quality of one's own thoughts or remembered experiences. Reflection on life's experiences takes on added meaning when learners share their "reflections" with others.

■ *Does the following activity make use of this guideline?*

Ask one member to give a brief report on Paul's viewpoint on faith.

_____ Yes

_____ No

The activity does not call for the learner to reflect on his own experiences. He tells of Paul's reflections on faith. You should have answered no.

■ *Does the following activity call for reflection on one's life experiences?*

Read aloud one by one the Beatitudes. After reading each, ask the group members to think in silence about the question: What does this verse say about my own life? What should I do or not do because of the truth in this verse?

_____ *Yes*

_____ *No*

The activity does call for learners to reflect upon their own lives.
Attitudes and values tend to change when learners reflect upon their own life experiences in the light of truth.

● Use activities like these to help learners reflect upon their own life experiences:

1. Read a short passage from the Bible. Then ask, What does this passage say to you about your own life? (Instead of, What does this passage mean?)

2. Ask questions which call for reflection. (For example: Write out your own conversion experience. What things have you done in your life which you now regret? What would you do differently if you could live the last year over? Write an essay on "If I Had Only Twenty-four Hours to Live."

3. On the chalkboard write a word such as "grace." Ask learners to describe what their life would be like without it.

4. Ask learners to make lists of their own strengths and weaknesses. Call on them to share their lists with the group if they desire.

9. *Arrange for learners to share their insights with others in a climate of freedom.*—Learners use this guideline when they take part in small groups whose members share their thoughts and feelings. Group leaders help create a climate of freedom when they guard against showing alarm at statements learners make; when they respect the dignity of persons. When done in a climate of acceptance and caring, sharing can shape attitudes and values.

Learners tend to change attitudes when they share insights in a climate of freedom.

■ *Would the following learning activity foster the sharing of insights with others in a climate of freedom?*

Announce the topic as "The World's Greatest Resource." Then divide members into groups of three. Ask each to tell the others (1) the most beautiful place I have ever seen, (2) the most meaningful experience I have ever had; (3) why____(name)____has meant more to me than any other person in this world. (Personal experiences of people become The World's Great Resource!) [2]

_____ Yes

_____ No

In small groups learners tend to feel more freedom in sharing. We believe the three questions would reveal insights and cause learners to reflect. We believe the answer you should have checked is "yes."

---

[2] Technique used by Ted Ward, Michigan State University.

■ *Would the following activity foster sharing of insights?*

Present to the pupils a thirty-minute slide presentation on "My Seven Wonders of the World."

_____ Yes

_____ No

Such an activity views of sharing as a one way street. It has value, but it does not call for true sharing of insight. You should have checked no.

262

Arrange for learners to share their insights and
reflections with others—in a climate of freedom!

"FORGIVE ME FOR TALKING ABOUT MYSELF SO MUCH! NOW **YOU** TALK ABOUT ME!"

Small groups tend to foster sharing of insights!

Sharing insights in a climate of freedom affects attitudes.

● Use activities such as these to help learners share insights in a climate of freedom.

1. Divide members into small sharing groups. Assign brief questions for discussion.

2. Ask each person to tell not only his name but an interesting experience.

3. Present a case study. Ask for opinions about how to handle the problem.

4. Conduct a "personal testimony" session—Quaker meeting style.

5. Ask learners to read silently a Bible passage. Ask them to share what they understand the verse to mean.

6. Lead a panel forum in which three persons discuss among themselves before the group a probing question. Allow group members to ask questions of the panel.

7. Ask learners to draw up a list of "life priorities" and to arrange them in order of importance.

CHECK YOUR PROGRESS

● In the space below, write in your own words the last group of five guidelines which relate to change in attitudes and values.

5. _____
   _____

6. _____
   _____

7. _____
   _____

8. _____
   _____

9. _____
   _____

Check your answers with the guidelines listed previously.

● For a review of the guidelines or principles of learning and how they involve learning activities, match the learning activities at the right with the guidelines of learning in the left-hand column. See if you can get seven of ten correct (*Note: One has two answers*).

Guidelines

Learning Activities

_____ Set a personal example

_____ Read or hear about persons who exemplify the attitude

_____ Provide for meaningful emotional experience

_____ Confront authoritative sources

_____ Take positive action

_____ Identify and define an attitude

_____ Practice making decisions on moral and ethical problems; analyze our values.

_____ Share insights with others in a climate of freedom

_____ Reflect upon their own life experiences

1. Ask three pupils to read aloud from three different dictionaries the definition of "love."
2. Read aloud the parable of the good Samaritan. Then ask, What attitude do you feel the parable deals with? Wait for answers.
3. Ask the pupils to study the autobiography, *How I Overcame Fear,* by John Doe.
4. Ask members in small groups to give personal testimonies on God's call.
5. Read Psalm 23 aloud. After each verse ask, What weaknesses in your own life does this verse call to mind?
6. Invite to the session a person who has successfully overcome tragedy. Ask him to give his personal testimony on "Triumph Through Tragedy."
7. Read to the group the report on "alcohol and health" produced by the surgeon general's office.
8. Ask each person to write a letter to a person who means a great deal to them. Ask them to tell the recipient why he has influenced their life.
9. Lead the members to do such things as the following to aid physically handicapped people: bring them to church, deliver wheelchairs, etc.
10. Ask, what would you do if a cashier gave you one dollar too much change?

Check your answers with these: 6, 3, 8, 7, 9, 1, 10, 4, 5. You may have given a few answers which differ from these.

● You have completed the section on teaching for change in attitudes and values. By now you have discovered that attitudes and values are the most difficult outcomes with which to work. Hopefully, this chapter has given you some helpful, practical ideas which you can use.

Unit 9 deals with the "levels of learning" which relate to attitudes and values.

UNIT 9

Levels of Attitudes and Values [1]

Why You Will Find This Study Useful:

Pupils need to learn facts and understand
what they mean. But more important, they
need to develop right attitudes and values.
They need to progress from "feeling" about
something to a life-style which reflects
day by day their attitudes and values.

The "indicators" of attitude change you will
learn to write in this unit will help you
judge the degree to which a pupil's attitude
has changed.

What You May Expect to Learn:

Goal: A study of this unit should help you
understand the process of writing learning
indicators at the levels of attitude learning
this unit presents.

Some Things You Will Do to Prove You Have Achieved This Goal:

 * Write indicators of learning at the five levels of
   attitude learning this unit presents.

 * Identify the level of learning (related to
   attitudes and values) which given indicators
   represent.

 * Match the five levels of learning related to
   attitudes and values with their explanations.

 * Recall the five levels of learning related to
   attitudes and values.

You will need approximately 45 minutes to complete this unit.

---

[1] *Taxonomy of Educational Objectives, Handbook II: Affective Domain,* D. R.
Krathwohl, B. S. Bloom, and B. B. Masia. David McKay Company, New York, 1964.
Adaptive use by permission of David McKay Company.

Preview of Terms Used in This Unit:

Life-style.—A manner of living which reflects day-by-day one's attitudes and values.

Receiving.—The level of attitude learning at which the learner simply becomes aware that a thing exists.

Responding.—The level of attitude learning at which the learner to some small degree commits himself to something. He has not acted on his feelings as yet.

Valuing.—The level of attitude learning at which the learner attaches worth to something. He commits himself to the extent that he pursues what he values.

Organization.—The level of attitude learning at which the learner brings several values to bear on a situation. He must decide which of several good things has priority.

Characterization.—The level of attitude learning at which the learner has a life-style which reflects day-by-day his attitude and values.

271

UNIT 9

Levels of Attitudes and Values

● Units 3 and 4 dealt with levels of learning related to knowledge and understanding. This unit deals with the levels of learning related to attitudes and values. It includes such kinds of learnings as appreciation, valuing, and so on. This kind of learning deals with a person's response to the content, the problem, or the area of experience. It depicts the human point of view toward a person, place, thing, or idea.

● As in the other kinds of learning, attitudes and values involve several levels. The levels appear below. The levels move from the simplest to the most complex. Each includes those before it. Read the explanations as a preview of the rest of this unit.

Receiving is the lowest level of attitudinal learning. At this level the learner simply becomes aware that something exists. It also suggests the willingness of the learner to receive. He focuses his attention on the thing or idea.

Responding, the second level, suggests that the learner goes beyond paying attention to a thing or idea. He may commit himself to some small degree to the thing he perceives. He does not take action as yet. He simply stops to ponder.

Valuing, the third level, suggests that the learner attaches *worth* to a person, thing, or idea. He reacts in a consistent way toward the thing, person, idea, and so on. The learner commits himself to persons and ideas which he believes have value. He commits himself to the extent that he pursues the thing valued. He may even reach the level of belief with a high degree of certainty. He believes in something strongly enough to "push" for it. He "talks" it.

Organization, the fourth level, suggests that he finds himself in situations which call for commitment to *more than one* value. He brings his values into a consistent system. His responses show that he has brought several values to bear on an event.

Characterization suggests that the learner acts at all times in the light of the values which have become his own. He has arrived at a consistent viewpoint toward life. He develops a life-style in keeping with his value system.

■ *Study the following chart which summarizes the levels of learning related to attitudes and values.*

CHARACTERIZATION   (The learner develops a style of life which reflects his total philosophy of life.)
ORGANIZATION   (The learner brings several values to bear on a situation.)
VALUING   (The learner commits himself to something because he sees value in it.)
RESPONDING   (The learner becomes interested in the subject.)
RECEIVING   (The learner becomes aware of something—a situation, idea, et cetera. He may even stop to pay attention to it.)

■ *Each of the following phrases suggests one of the levels of learning shown. Rank them in order. Assign number 1 to the level of receiving and so on. Refer to the preceding chart if necessary.*

_____ *develops a system of values*

_____ *becomes aware of persons, places, ideas, and stops to pay attention*

_____ *practices what he preaches*

_____ *attaches worth to persons, places, ideas, and so on, commits himself to a point of view*

_____ *does something with or about the thing received; stops to consider or ponder*

You probably answered with the following sequence: four, one, five, three, two.

■ *The next exercise will require a lot of thinking. Try it. It will help clarify the five levels.*

A part of the biography of missionary Robert Moffat dramatizes several of these levels. Read this excerpt from his biography. Then answer the questions which follow the excerpt.

It was after Robert had left his home in Scotland and begun work as a gardener on a large estate at High Leigh, England, that one summer evening he sat out intending to make some purchases in the shops . . . . He crossed the bridge that led into Warrington and came to a sudden halt before a poster that hung by the roadside. Mastered by a curiosity he could not explain, he read the words once and again: "Missionary Meeting. Guild Hall, Warrington, Thursday Evening, July 25. Speaker, Reverend William Roby, of Manchester." The date was past, the meeting over, and the speaker already departed to his home. What invisible hand wove the spell that held young Robert Moffat rooted to the spot, oblivious to all around him?

By a quick process of association the words awakened memories that had been for a long time slumbering in the young man's mind.

Then all at once, he understood why the placard, with its notice of a bygone event, stirred such a commotion in his mind. God was calling him, Robert Moffat, to the life of a missionary, exactly as he had called the men and women of the Moravian church years before. He committed himself to God's call and served many fruitful years as a missionary to South Africa. [2]

Which phrase suggests the level of receiving?

_____

Which phrase suggests the level of responding?

_____

Which phrase suggests the level of valuing?

_____

Which phrase suggests the level of characterization?

_____

[2] Ethel Daniels Hubbard, *The Moffats* (New York: Friendship Press, 1944), pp. 21–23. Used by permission.

You may have chosen the following; however, we asked for your opinion:

Receiving: "came to a sudden halt before a poster."

Responding: "he read the words once and again."

Valuing: "God was calling him"; "He committed himself."

Characterization: "served many fruitful years as a missionary to South Africa."

Perhaps some phrases suggest the level we omitted—organization of a value system, but they do not stand out as much as the others.

CHECK YOUR PROGRESS

■ *In the following activity, match each level of learning with its definition. (One of the levels will have two answers.)*

_____ Characterization

_____ Organization

_____ Valuing

_____ Responding

_____ Receiving

1. *The learner sees the worth and value of something. He commits himself to the idea.*

2. *The learner becomes aware that a thing exists. He is willing to receive it.*

3. *A learner acts at all times in keeping with his value system. His life-style reflects his values.*

4. *A learner bases his decisions on several values instead of one.*

5. *The learner does more than become aware of something. He pays attention and may commit himself to some small degree.*

6. *A learner notices something and makes a mental note of what he saw.*

Check your answers against these: 3, 4, 1, 5, 2 and 6. (The last one has two answers: 2 and 6.)

Indicators of Attitude Change

● As in the other areas of learning—knowledge, understanding, and skills—teachers can write goals and indicators in areas of attitudes and values. In previous units you have seen some of them. The statement which follows also appears in Unit Two. Read it two or three times. Study it carefully. Note the goal and the three *indicators*:

The learner demonstrates an attitude of compassion for the emotional needs of retarded children. To demonstrate achievement of the goal, the learner *consistently* does such things as:

1. Volunteers to teach in the special education department.

2. Reads a book on emotional needs of children.

3. Baby-sits with retarded children.

■ *Study the three indicators. Assume that a learner did such things day in and day out. At which level of learning would you place him?*

_____ *Characterization*

_____ *Organization*

_____ *Valuing*

_____ *Responding*

_____ *Receiving*

You see, the indicators in the example say that the learner took three actions—volunteered, read, and baby-sat. If the learner devotes his life to doing the kinds of things listed, we would say he had reached the level of characterization. He did more than just pay attention to the need (Responding). He felt commitment of such strength that he did something specific about it. But he did many things day in and day out. It became his life style. We believe that the word "consistently" suggests the level of characterization.

278

● How does one arrive at indicators of attitudes and values? Ideas for indicators of attitude change do not come as easily as those for other kinds of learning. But the suggestion which follows should help:

Read again the goal: "The learner demonstrates an attitude of compassion for the emotional needs of retarded children." The teacher may ask, "Assume that one could observe in real life a person whose life-style showed commitment to meeting the emotional needs of retarded persons. Assume, also that one could follow such a person during an entire day or week. If the observer made a list of things the committed person *did* during the day, what would he see on the list? For example: "I saw John Doe enrolling in a college course in special education. I saw John Doe offer to take a group of children for a walk in the zoo. I saw John Doe sharing with parents of retarded children a new book on *Living with Special Children*." And so on. These observations can become typical indicators. They tell what the learner does to show that he has the attitude.

But indicators of attitude differ in one significant way from indicators of knowledge, understanding, and skills. *The learner needs to do them voluntarily to indicate he has changed.* As a rule the teacher does not post a list of attitudinal indicators as he would when teaching for knowledge or understanding. He simply waits for the learner to respond of his own free will in the ways (or like ways).

The pages which follow will help you recognize indicators of attitude change at the five levels.

Receiving—At the level of *receiving* the learner becomes aware that an idea, person, or thing exists. He may not give attention to it. He shows *willingness to receive* a given idea as opposed to avoiding it. He may even focus attention on the subject.

■ **Which of the following indicators suggest(s) the level of receiving?**

_____ 1. *The learner, while passing down the hall, notices a poster depicting "world hunger."*

_____ 2. *The learner listens while someone else talks about "world hunger."*

_____ 3. *Both 1 and 2.*

_____ 4. *Neither 1 nor 2.*

The learner "received" in both examples. He receives the image and message on the poster. If one should ask what he saw, he could say he saw a poster on "hunger." In number 2, the learner showed a willingness to receive. You should have checked number 3.

Number 1 (noticing the poster) suggests that teachers display such posters, hoping that persons will take notice. The teacher cannot control to any large degree the "receiving." She or he simply displays the poster or talks about "world hunger." The display "invites" the learner to receive.

● *Responding*—At this level the learner does more than give attention. He becomes mentally active in regard to the subject. He has real interest in the subject. He complies with rules but has not fully accepted the need for doing so. He has not formed a deep commitment as yet. He simply shows his interest.

■ **Which of the following indicators suggest(s) the level of responding?**

_____ **1. On "Christian Vocation Day" the learner answers an invitation to dedicate himself to the study of medicine.**

_____ **2. Seeing in the hall a poster on "World Hunger," the learner stops, turns toward the poster and ponders it momentarily.**

_____ **3. Both 1 and 2.**

_____ **4. Neither 1 nor 2.**

Item two suggests the level of responding. Item one suggests a high level (valuing) in which the learner commits himself to the subject.

● *Valuing.*—This level suggests that the learner commits himself to the idea or subject. He has already focused attention on the subject; he has done something with or about the subject. But he has gone further. He has decided that the subject has worth and merit. He "prefers" the idea. He deepens his involvement.

■ **Which of these indicators suggest(s) the level of valuing? (Commits himself.)**

_____ **1. The learner talks often about the importance of Christian social services.**

_____ **2. The learner signs a tithe card.**

_____ **3. Both 1 and 2.**

_____ **4. Neither 1 nor 2.**

We believe you should have checked item three. Both suggest valuing. In number 1 the learner shows, a definite preference for Christian social services. He seeks out ways to promote the cause. In number 2 the learner has come to the point at which he commits himself to tithe. He has seen its worth to the extent that he makes a personal commitment to tithing.

● *Organization.*—At the "organization" level the learner must ponder two or more values. More than one value may apply. For example, a driver of a car needed to arrive at a conference on time. He wanted to set the example. By turning left in a "no left turn" intersection, he could have arrived on time. However, to turn left would place human lives in jeopardy. In addition, obedience to the law flashed through his mind. He decided not to turn left because the "worth" of human lives and violation of a law superseded his concept of the worth of "being on time."

The learner sees how a value relates to those he already holds or to new values. His values come into an ordered relationship with one another. He can answer problem situations by assessing the relative values of many approaches each of which has value.

■ **Which of these indicators represent the level of organization?**

_____ **1. The learner works out a plan for regulating his rest in relation to the demands of his work activities.**

_____ **2. The learner notices a "No Smoking" sign.**

_____ **3. Both 1 and 2.**

_____ **4. Neither 1 nor 2.**

Item one suggests a system of values—it indicates the learner valued or "worthed" both his rest needs and his work needs. He pondered the two needs. He came up with a plan which would allow him to attach appropriate worth to both. In number 2, the learner simply "received." He did not even respond. He had not fully accepted the "values" of not smoking. He did not relate one value to another. In other words, he did not say, "Since the law says not to smoke, and since smoking may injure my health, I will stop smoking." You should have checked number one.

OR Daddy, get your value system organized!

● *Characterization.*—At this level, the learner has organized his values into a system in keeping with his convictions. His convictions control his way of acting to the extent that he behaves in keeping with his values. He has developed a philosophy of life which has meaning. His life-style matches his values. Other persons say that his life-style reflects his system of values.

■ *Which of these indicators reflect(s) the level of characterization?*

_____ 1. *"Jesus went about doing good."*

_____ 2. *The learner says, "Since joining your group my entire world view has changed, and I'm trying to live accordingly."*

_____ 3. *Both 1 and 2.*

_____ 4. *Neither 1 nor 2.*

You should have checked item three. Both the statements indicate life-style and philosophy of life.

CHECK YOUR PROGRESS

● And now for review, match the statements at the right with the level of learning in the left hand column. (Note: It is possible that not all the statements apply).

Level of Learning

_____ Characterization

_____ Organization

_____ Valuing

_____ Responding

_____ Receiving

Statement

1. I stop and pay attention to something I have seen or heard. I consider seriously the thing I observe.

2. I recognize and accept the worth of something. I believe in it enough to "push" for it. I'm committed to it.

3. Day in and day out my life-style reflects my value system.

4. I become aware through my senses that something exists.

5. I can assess relative values and make decisions which call for consideration of several values I hold.

6. I perform an act as the trainer demonstrates.

We believe the best order is 3, 5, 2, 1, 4. Number 6 does not belong in the attitudinal area—it relates more to motor skill development.

**MOTOR SKILL
OUTCOMES**

UNIT 10

How to Peel Your Own Bananas
(Learning Activities to Develop Motor Skills)

Why You Will Find the Study Useful:

Many times you will need to train a person to do
    a motor skill—like beating time patterns in music,
    or tying a knot. The learning activities you will
    learn to design will help you train the pupil in
    less time. What he learns will last longer, too.

What You May Expect to Learn:

Goal.—A study of this unit should help you understand how
    to design learning activities to help persons learn motor skills.

Some Things You Will Do to Prove You Have Achieved This Goal:

    * Design learning activities to use in training
      persons to perform a motor skill.

    * Identify the principles of learning (guidelines)
      a given skills activity employs

    * List and explain the guidelines for motor skills
      training this unit presents.

You will need about 45 minutes to complete this unit.

Preview of Terms Used in This Unit.

Motor skill.—A skill which requires one to perform a physical act with ease—like riding a bicycle.

Psychomotor skill.—Another term for motor skill.

Demonstration.—The performance of an act so that a learner may watch the process.

Realistic conditions.—Conditions similar to those under which a person will perform an act in real life.

UNIT 10

"How to Peel Your Own Bananas"
(Learning Activities to Develop Motor Skills)

● Motor skill means the ability to perform a physical act well or with ease. A person who walks a tightrope, weaves a basket, or plays a piano uses motor skills.

Planning learning activities to develop motor skills assumes that the learning goal and indicator call for a motor skill. For example: The learner demonstrates *skill* in peeling shrimp by peeling three dozen shrimp in ten minutes. The learning goal calls for *skill* in a motor activity. We call these "psychomotor skills." "Perceptual" (nonmotor) skills relate to knowledge and understanding. One uses "perceptual skill" to plan a lesson, write a novel or solve a problem.

■ *Which of the following represents a motor skill?*

_____ *1. Riding a bicycle*

_____ *2. Quoting a verse of Scripture*

Item one requires motor skill primarily. Item two involves a "perceptual" skill; not a motor skill.

Several guidelines for teaching and training relate in a special way to motor skills training. Teachers who want to help learners acquire a motor skill provide learning activities which apply the guidelines or principles for developing these skills.

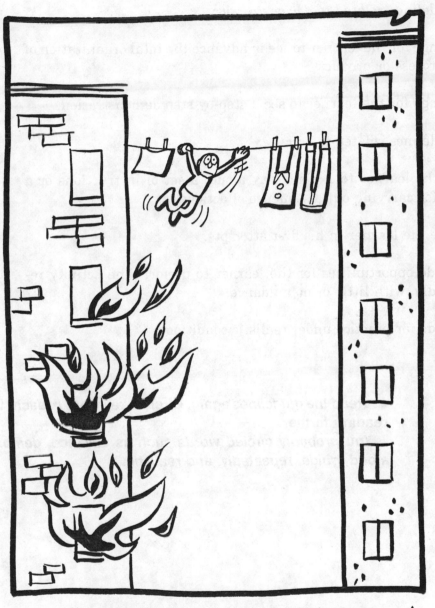

YOU NEVER KNOW WHEN YOU WILL NEED A MOTOR SKILL!

● To help you "see in advance" six guidelines which in a special way apply to developing motor skills, read this list. Note that the guidelines fall into two main groups—one group relates to demonstration-observation. The other relates to practice.

The guidelines related to *demonstration:*

1. Arrange for the learner to see in advance the total organization of the process or product.

2. Arrange for the learner to see a step-by-step demonstration.

The guidelines related to *practice:*

3. Ask the learner to explain (say aloud) a set of instructions or a plan for carrying out a sequence of actions.

4. Guide the learner in his first attempts.

5. Provide opportunities for the learner to perform the activity repeatedly, with little or no guidance.

6. Provide for practice under realistic conditions.

■ *Read the guidelines again. Circle a key word in each.* Do this before reading further.
    You probably circled words such as advance, demonstration, say aloud, guide, repeatedly, and realistic.

● The material which follows presents one at a time the guidelines for developing motor skills.

1. The guidelines related to demonstration.

(1) *Arrange for the learner to see in advance the total process or product.*—Trainers use this guideline or principle when they show charts which picture how to do something. They use it when they show a handcraft class a hooked rug (completed product) *before* teaching how to do it.

Learners tend to develop motor skills more efficiently when they see in advance the total organization of the process or the product.

The principle of advance organization applies to all learning outcomes.[1] It applies to knowledge and understanding outcomes as well. In skill development the learner needs to see a complete performance of an act before he begins it himself. When he observes a complete demonstration, he gets some idea of the kinds of things he will need to learn to do. The learner sees an example of the end result before beginning. He observes a model of what he will learn to do. *At this point, the leader does not stop to explain how to perform the steps.* A good demonstration provides an overview of the skill. Some skills result in products one can see and touch. For example, tying a knot results in a tied knot. Seeing a tied knot at the beginning of a knot-tying session should help the learner learn more readily. He tends to learn better if he sees in advance the total product or the result of the skill.

---

[1] Research on the value of advance organizers has resulted in differing opinions as to their value. This writer has found them helpful.

■ Which of the following call(s) for the use of advance organization in motor skill development? (Ask, Does the pupil see the completed product before he begins work? Does he observe the complete process before doing it himself?)

_____ 1. A teacher of basket weaving asked the students to make a basket as she demonstrated step by step.

_____ 2. A teacher of basket weaving displayed a completed basket. She pointed out the different patterns the pupils would learn to weave.

_____ 3. Both 1 and 2.

_____ 4. Neither 1 nor 2.

Number 2 makes use of advance organization. The learners see in advance the product of the skill. In number 1 the teacher has not used an advance organizer. The student makes the basket with neither the benefit of seeing the finished product nor of seeing the complete process.

■ Use activities like these to help the learner see (or hear) in advance the total process or product:

1. Show a film which shows a total process.

2. Show the learner a machine in operation.

3. Show a chart which outlines all the steps in an operation.

4. Display a completed product, such as a woven basket.

5. Play an entire anthem before teaching the voice parts.

6. Play a recording of a piece of piano music before starting practice.

(2) *Arrange for the learner to observe a demonstration step by step.*—A trainer showed a film on how to build a canoe. The film showed and explained fifteen steps to master in the process. The trainer "arranged" for the learner to observe a step-by-step demonstration.

Learners tend to develop motor skills more efficiently when they follow a demonstration step by step.

The pupils observe demonstrations of each step, as the leader explains. They ask questions if necessary. Mastery of a complex skill calls for mastery of the subskills involved. Step-by-step demonstration allows time for the learner to focus the steps in a process. Demonstrations by the leader have more effect when the leader explains as he shows. Mistakes conveyed through one of the senses are corrected by what one receives through other senses.

■ *Which of the following allow(s) the learner to see a step-by-step demonstration?*

_____ *1. In a course in learning aids, class members viewed a slide set on how to use the overhead projector. The material broke down the process into ten critical steps.*

_____ *2. In a driver's training class, the school did not have a dual control automobile. Instead the trainer drove the car. The student watched and listened as the trainer explained how to parallel park.*

_____ *3. Both 1 and 2.*

_____ *4. Neither 1 nor 2.*

You should have checked number 3. Both call for the learner to follow a demonstration step-by-step. Number 1 provides a slide demonstration; number 2 a live one with comments. Both call for step-by-step observation.

● In the space below, write the first two guidelines related to skills.

1. _____
   _____

2. _____
   _____

To check your answers, refer to the list of guidelines just studied.

● To make use of step-by-step demonstration, use activities like these.

1. Divide class into groups of two persons. One shows the other how to do a skill.

2. Show a film which shows and tells step-by-step.

3. Do a large group demonstration—use an overhead transparency to illustrate steps.

● 2. The guidelines related to practice.

You have studied two guidelines related to demonstration of skills. Consider now four guidelines and principles related to practice.

(3) *Ask the learner to explain (say aloud) a set of instructions or a plan for doing something.*—A trainer said to a trainee, "Now, you tell me how to assemble the clock. You teach and I'll learn!" The trainee orally explained each step. In the process he taught himself.

Learners tend to develop skill more efficiently when they verbalize (say aloud) a set of instructions or a plan for carrying out a sequence of actions.

In this kind of activity the learner tests his own understanding of what he needs to do. He tries to express with words the steps in doing it. Though not actual practice, verbalization serves as a double check. It assures the learner that he has the sequence of steps in mind.

■ *A teacher gave the following instructions. Which one calls for the learner to verbalize what he should do?*

_____ *1. Now, drive the stakes through the loops.*

_____ *2. Now, tell me in your own words what you should do in each step.*

_____ *3. Lift the lever according to the instructions.*

Number 2 calls for the learner to verbalize or to describe a process in his own words. In the other two, the trainer simply gives directions for doing an act.

● Learners verbalize instructions when they do activities such as these:

1. Write or narrate a slide set on the steps in a process.

2. Explain as another person performs.

3. Explain the process to the trainer.

4. Read instructions aloud as they perform.

● (4) *Guide the learner in his first attempts.*—A shorthand teacher wrote comments on practice homework done by pupils. A mechanic watched as the learner repaired brakes on a car. A choir director stopped the choir at the end of a measure and pointed out ways to improve. All made use of the principle of guiding learners in their first attempts.

Learners tend to develop skills more efficiently when they receive guidance on first attempts.

Guidance on first attempts helps correct errors early. Repeating errors tends to cause one to learn the errors. Guidance provides feedback. It provides the learner with knowledge of results. This guideline grows out of the principle of immediate knowledge of results. If the learner knows immediately that he has done something correctly, he will more than likely do it correctly again. The "guide" both corrects mistakes and praises for correct responses.

■ **Which of these activities show(s) that the trainer gave guidance on first attempts?**

_____ 1. **A trainer showed a trainee how to splice and edit audiotapes. She then asked the students to go to the control room and edit given tapes. A week later each student played for the class an edited tape.**

_____ 2. **A trainer showed and explained how to clean a tape recorder. He then asked the students to perform step one in cleaning the recorder. As the students performed, the trainer watched the group members, and called attention to steps they omitted or did incorrectly.**

_____ 3. **Both 1 and 2.**

_____ 4. **Neither 1 nor 2.**

In item one the pupils had no guidance from the trainer. They practiced in the control room but without guidance. In number 2, the teacher observed the performances and pointed out mistakes. You should have checked number two.

■ *Which of these activities employ(s) the principle of guidance on first attempts?*

_____ 1. *To introduce a training session on how to use the lathe to produce "turned" legs for furniture, the trainer displayed several turned pieces, ranging from simple to complex.*

_____ 2. *In a class in woodwork, the trainer followed his demonstration by asking a student to insert a 2 x 2 piece of lumber in his own lathe. As the student produced a simple round table leg, the trainer reminded him to fasten the safety device.*

_____ 3. *Both 1 and 2.*

_____ 4. *Neither 1 nor 2.*

You should have checked item two. The trainer in number 2 gave guidance. In number one the trainer used another principle—advance organization. Guided response reflects the "guided response" level of learning.

301

■ *Now try to write in your own words the first four guidelines for skills training.*

1. _____
   _____

2. _____
   _____

3. _____
   _____

4. _____
   _____

Check your answers with the statements at the beginning of this unit.

● To guide learners on first attempts, use activities such as these:

1. Use programmed instruction devices which give immediate knowledge of results.

2. Ask each person to show you how to perform the act. Correct mistakes and give "praise" for correct response.

3. Assign "training helpers" to work with the group members on a one-to-one basis.

4. Ask learners to record on a tape and play it back to discover their own errors.

● (5) *Provide opportunities for the learner to perform the act repeatedly, with little or no guidance.*—A trainer "put the trainees on their own." They practiced over and over. They knew the trainer would help only if needed. They used the principle of repeated performance.

Learners tend to develop skills more efficiently when they perform the activity repeatedly, without guidance.

A learner who repeats an act forms motor habits. He learns to perform the act with little forethought. He performs on his own. He judges for himself the correctness of his work. He develops speed and accuracy. The sub-skills become habitual. He overlearns the skill. He retains the ability even after a lapse of time. He does not have to think in order to know what to do next.

■ **Which of the following situations call(s) for the learner to repeat a performance?**

_____ 1. **In a class in shorthand, the teacher provided each day a period in which students wrote from three-minute segments of dictation tape. The material required the use of the new characters they had learned during the unit. They wrote each three-minute segment six times.**

_____ 2. **In a class in shorthand, the teacher illustrated the new characters by writing them on the chalkboard. Then she wrote sentences using the characters. She then projected on the screen a correct copy. Students corrected their dictation using the projected copy as a guide.**

Repetition involves repetition of the same activity. You should have checked number 1. In number 2 the learners did many things, but they did not repeat an activity.

304

● Make use of the guideline related to repeated performance in such ways as these:

1. Provide lab periods for practice.

2. Assign "homework" practice.

3. Conduct "speed drills" in course where learners need speed.

4. Set "goals" for speed or accuracy (in track and basketball, free throws for example).

● (6) *Provide for practice under realistic conditions.*—A pilot practiced in a "flight simulator." He practiced under realistic conditions.

Learners tend to develop motor skills more efficiently when they practice under conditions which approximate reality.

The trainer provides real life or made-up situations in which the learner practices. Swimmers learn to swim in water. They practice in the environment in which they will perform. Difficulty in providing real life practice has lead to the widespread use of simulation and academic games in training. Astronauts practice in simulated situations because they cannot practice in the real life environment until later. But the situation comes as close to real life as possible. The trainer avoids the use of makeshift or substitute equipment when possible.

■ **Which of the following situations call(s) for practice under realistic conditions?**

_____ 1. **After much practice of an anthem in the choir room, with piano only, the director of music moved the choir to the concert hall where they practiced with an orchestra.**

_____ 2. **In a class in office practice, the trainer arranged for the class members to serve as secretaries to the other teachers for two hours each week.**

_____ 3. **In a class in mechanics, students overhauled a motor in the school's model shop.**

You probably checked all three. All the situations call for practice under real life conditions. Numbers one and two call for the learner to perform "on location." Number 3 takes place in a "mock-up" of the actual place. However, model shops come close to real life.

306

● Activities such as these provide for practice in realistic conditions.

1. Use "driving simulators" to teach driving. Or better still, drive one hundred miles!

2. Practice for recitals in the concert hall.

3. Do auto repair in a garage.

4. Use a vocational training approach in which students train part of the day and work in an office or factory part of the day.

● For purposes of review, match the following situations with the guidelines involved.

_____ 1. Students in secretarial science changed typewriter ribbons in all the school offices.

_____ 2. Students practiced changing typewriter ribbons in class until they could perform the operation in 45 seconds.

_____ 3. Students viewed a film on steps in changing a typewriter ribbon.

_____ 4. Students changed ribbons on their own typewriters while the trainer circulated among them confirming or correcting as necessary.

_____ 5. Students viewed a picture of the ribbon mechanism of a typewriter.

_____ 6. Students gathered around the teacher and watched her change a ribbon.

_____ 7. As each student changed a ribbon on his own typewriter, he explained to the trainer each step.

1. Arrange for the learner to see in advance the total organization of the process or product.

2. Arrange for the learner to see a step-by-step demonstration.

3. Ask the learner to explain (say aloud) a set of instructions or a plan for carrying out a sequence of actions.

4. Guide the learner in his first attempts.

5. Provide opportunities for the learner to perform the activity repeatedly, with little or no guidance.

6. Provide for practice under realistic conditions.

With some room for argument, the following sequence seems to provide the best answers: 6, 5, 2, 4, 1, 2, and 3.

Practice under realistic conditions reflects all five of the levels of skills learning. Regardless of when or how the learner practices, he needs to practice in real life situations.

Unit 11 will present the levels of learning in the area of motor skills.

UNIT 11

How to Really Peel Your Own Bananas
(Levels of Learning in Motor Skill Development)

Why You Will Find the Study Useful:

Pupils who need to develop motor skills
come into training with differing degrees
of background in the skill.

Teachers and trainers need to find out where
to begin in teaching motor skills to persons
who come into training with differing degrees
of background in the skill.

This unit will help you decide "where to begin" with each learner
in teaching motor skills

What You May Expect to Learn:

Goal: A study of this unit should help you understand the levels of
learning in the area of motor skills.

Some Things You Will Do to Prove You Have Achieved This Goal:

* Write indicators of motor skill development
at the levels of learning which this unit presents.

* Classify a list of indicators as to the level of
motor skills learning each suggests.

* List and explain the five levels of learning
related to motor skills.

You will need about 40 minutes to complete this unit.

Preview of Terms Used in This Unit:

Perception.—The level of motor skill learning at which a learner becomes aware of something through the senses.

Set.—The level of motor skill learning at which the learner gets himself "ready" or "set" to act.

Guided Response.—The level of motor skills learning at which the learner performs an act, but does so under guidance.

Habit.—The level of motor skills learning at which a learner masters to the point of habit, a point of a complex skill.

Complex Overt Response.—The highest level of motor skill learning at which the learner performs with a high degree of skill a complex activity.

UNIT 11

"How to Really Peel Your Own Bananas"
(Levels of Learning in Motor Skill Development) [1]

● Other units have dealt with the levels of learning which relate to knowledge, understanding, and attitudes. Motor skills also have levels of complexity. This unit deals with the levels of learning related to motor skills. Educators have not identified the skills levels as clearly as they have the levels of knowledge and understanding.

Motor skills require more than knowledge, understanding, and a good attitude! They require a high degree of coordination of the muscles. Like the other learning outcomes we may think of levels of motor skills learning. Notice the five levels shown in the following chart.

COMPLEX OVERT RESPONSE **(The learner performs with a high degree of** **skill a complex activity.)**
HABIT (MECHANISM) **(The learner masters to the point of "habit"** **a part of a complex skill.)**
GUIDED RESPONSE **(The learner responds under guidance of a** **teacher or trainer.)**
SET **(The learner gets mentally and physically** **"set," or ready to act.)**
PERCEPTION **(The learner becomes aware through his senses.)**

---

[1] Adapted from Elizabeth Simpson, *Taxonomy of Objectives: Psychomotor Domain,* 1968. (Unpublished paper), University of Illinois, Urbana. Used by permission.

When one learns a motor skill he first perceives or becomes aware of something through his senses. He touches, hears, smells, tastes, or sees it. We call this first level the level of *perception*.

In the second level the learner's mind, body, and emotions become ready to do an act. He has not only become aware of a skill; he has developed readiness or a "set" to respond to what he has perceived. We call this the level of *"set."*

In the third level the learner, under guidance, begins to perform the sub-skills of the skill. He does not as yet perform the complex act. We call this the level of *guided response*.

In the fourth level the learner gains confidence through practice. He performs the sub-skills with a little thought. The act becomes habitual. He has the sub-skill in his bag of tricks. He can use it when called upon to do a more complex act. We call this the level of *mechanism*.

In the fifth level the learner at last performs with a high degree of ease a complex skill. He makes a complex overt response. We call this the level of *complex overt response*.

Some learnings require more than knowledge
and understanding!

"I KNOW MY LEVEL OF COMPETENCY"

■ *The levels of skills learning progress from the simple to the complex. Which of the following would you consider the more complex psychomotor skill?*

_____ 1. *The learner plays "The Flight of the Bumble Bee" on the violin.*

_____ 2. *The learner learns to draw the bow across the strings of a violin so as to produce a clear tone.*

Number 1 requires a more complex skill. It involves not only bowing the violin, but fingering, interpreting, and so on.

● The motor skills aspect of learning involves reaction and coordination of muscles. It may include handling of materials or objects.

In the motor skills area the levels overlap just as they do in the other outcomes. But we separate them to help us think more clearly. As in the other learning outcomes the levels give us clues as to the kinds of goals, indicators, learning activities, and tests to use. Teachers can choose to write indicators (objectives) to require a skill response at given levels. They can design learning activities which call for action at given levels. Let's explore in greater depth what the five levels of motor skills learning mean.

1. *The level of perception.*—The lowest level, perception, constitutes the first step in performing a motor act. The learner becomes aware of objects, qualities, or relations by way of the senses. It may also involve "having an idea" of what to do as a result of becoming aware of something through the senses. For example, in basketball, the learner simply becomes aware that he will have to throw the ball in order to make a basket.

Clues to the perception level include (1) awareness through the senses or (2) recognition of hints or symptoms.

■ **Which of the following indicators would you classify at the perception level?**

_____ 1. *A student repairs a motor in shop class.*

_____ 2. *In shop class, a student hears an unusual noise in a motor and decides it needs tuning.*

_____ 3. *Both 1 and 2.*

_____ 4. *Neither 1 nor 2.*

Item two calls for awareness through the senses. In this case the learner heard the noise. He knew the motor did not run properly and that it needed repair. He "heard" and "got an idea." As yet he may not have learned how to repair it. You should have checked number two.

2. *The level of set.*—"Set" means "readiness" to do an act. The learner "readies" his mind, body, and emotions. At this time he focuses on *parts* of a complex skill. The learner focuses his mind on the subject—ready to act. He gets his body in the proper position to perform the act. Emotionally, he feels favorable toward doing the act. As yet he has not performed the act. He has become aware (perception) through his senses, and he has developed a readiness to do the act.

■ *Which of these indicators (objectives) call(s) for response at the level of "set"?*

_____ 1. *The learner assumes the proper stance for doing free throws in basketball.*

_____ 2. *Students paddle a canoe one mile through rough water.*

Item two involves the learner in doing a very complex action. Paddling a canoe requires learning of many sub-skills and the ability to combine them into a complex act. The learner has already passed the "set" level and the "perception" level. He has arrived at the highest level—complex overt response.

You should have checked number one. One suggests readiness of mind, body, and emotions. The learner has passed the perception level and has readied himself to begin to act. With ball in hand he gets ready and "set" to perform the act.

● 3. *The level of guided response.*—Here the teacher guides the student verbally or physically in performing the sub-skills of a complex skill. Or he may guide the learner in his first attempts at doing a complex act. The learner does not have to master all sub-skills before performing a complex one. Sometimes learners acquire certain skills more readily when they attempt a *complex* skill first. For example, research shows that in juggling three balls, best results come when the learner practices the whole act as he begins. He attempts to juggle the three balls rather than one, then two, and finally three. On the other hand, to gain skill in playing football the learner would practice first the sub-skills: passing, tackling, running, and blocking. Then the player would put these together in a game. In both cases the learner responds by practicing. The trainer gives advice and provides knowledge of results. With guidance the learner can perform the skill in the right way—perhaps not with ease—but in the right way.

■ *Which of the following excerpts from class session call(s) for response at the level of "guided response"?*

_____ 1. **Teacher:** *"Now, please attempt to replace the filmstrip holder with the slide holder in this projector."*

Student: *(begins to take steps necessary to make the change)*

Teacher: *"That's right, you did that step correctly."*

_____ 2. **Teacher:** *"Now, please attempt to replace the filmstrip holder with the slide holder in this projector."*

Student: *(begins to take steps necessary to make the change)*

Teacher: *"You did not unscrew the holder completely. That's why you could not remove it."*

_____ 3. **Both 1 and 2.**

_____ 4. **Neither 1 nor 2.**

You should have checked three. In both one and two the students responded under guidance. In number 1 the teacher reassured the student by commending a correct response. In number 2 the teacher guided the response. He told the student of the mistake and showed how to correct it.

321

■ **Which of the following indicators (objectives) call for response at the level of guided response?**

_____ 1. **The learner correctly threads a projector in fifteen seconds without the aid of a user's guide.**

_____ 2. **The learner threads a projector. He follows the steps shown in the user's guide.**

_____ 3. **Both 1 and 2.**

_____ 4. **Neither 1 nor 2.**

In item two the user's guide serves as "tutor." As a result the learner responds under guidance. You should have checked number 2. In number 1 the learner has passed beyond the need for a guide.

322

● 4. *The level of habit (mechanism).*—At this level the learner has practiced until his response has become habitual. He does not as yet perform a motor act which one would call complex. In a sense he performs "sub-skills" without guidance. He can perform without guidance, but has not achieved a high degree of ease in doing it. He has gained a degree of confidence and skill in doing an act. Clues to response at the level of habit (mechanism) include (1) performance without guidance; (2) performance of a moderately complex sub-skill; (3) and performance which has *not* reached the level of highly automatic response.

■ **Which of the following indicators call for learning at the level of mechanism?**

_____ **1. The learner sails a sailboat into a twenty-mile-an-hour wind without capsizing.**

_____ **2. In basketball, the player makes twenty-five points in a game.**

_____ **3. Both 1 and 2.**

_____ **4. Neither 1 nor 2.**

You should have answered number 4. Sailing, and making twenty-five points in a basketball game require learning of complex skills.

■ **Which of the following indicators call(s) for learning at the level of habit (mechanism)?**

_____ 1. The learner neatly hand hems a pair of trousers.

_____ 2. The learner tailors a suit for men.

_____ 3. Both 1 and 2.

_____ 4. Neither 1 nor 2.

Number 1 calls for response at the level of habit. Number 2 requires highly complex response. It calls for mastery of many sub-skills.
The difference between the levels of habit (mechanism) and complex overt response (the next level) is one of degree. They differ in the degree of complexity of the skill and the degree to which the learner performs without having to think.

324

5. *The level of complex overt responses.*—At this stage, the performance of the motor skill has become automatic. The learner performs a complex act with ease and a great deal of muscle control. The learner does not have to ponder what he should do next. Clues to complex overt response include (1) performance of a complex act; (2) automatic performance; and (3) absence of uncertainty.

■ **Which of the following activities call for response at the level of complex overt response?**

_____ 1. *A student in home economics tailors a suit.*

_____ 2. *A student in voice sings the soprano arias from Messiah.*

_____ 3. *A student of piano plays Debussy's "Claire de Lune."*

You should have checked all three. Each calls for a complex response done with ease.

CHECK YOUR PROGRESS

For review, list and explain the five levels of motor skills learning. Write the lowest level at the bottom; the highest at the top.

Level	Explanation
5.	
4.	
3.	
2.	
1.	

Check your answers with the chart at the first of this unit.

● Now, match the activities and indicators at the right with the level of learning shown at the left.

Levels of Skills Learning

_____ Complex overt response

_____ Habit (mechanism)

_____ Guided response

_____ Set

_____ Perception

Indicators

1. The learner squares and saws a one-by-twelve piece of lumber three feet long.

2. The learner assumes the proper stance on the diving board before making a backward dive.

3. The learner produces as a semester project in furniture design a three-piece bedroom set.

4. The learner notices a loose screw on a motor mount.

5. The learner positions his fingers in the proper position on a typewriter keyboard.

6. The learner installs an electrical outlet as the instructor watches and advises.

The answers are as follows: three, one, six, two and five, four.

EVALUATION

OF

LEARNING

UNIT 12

Explain the Universe and Give Two Good Examples!

(Evaluation of Learning and Instruction)

Why You Will Find This Study Useful:

The test questions you will learn to construct
   in this unit will help you devise tests
   which will do a better job of telling you
   whether the pupil has achieved the
   learning goals.

What You May Expect to Learn:

Goal: A study of this unit should help you understand the
   process of test construction and evaluation of learning.

Some Things You Will Do to Prove You Have Achieved This Goal:

> *General:*

* Define test

* Explain how tests relate to indicators.

> *Regarding Knowledge and Understanding:*

* Construct test items which match the goal-indicator
   statements as to form, content, and level of learning

* Match test items with the levels of learning related to
   knowledge and understanding.

330

* List the three ways in which a test item must match a goal indicator statement.

Regarding Attitudes and Values:

* Explain what "voluntary response" means

* Explain what "representative response" means.

You will need about 45 minutes to complete this unit.

Preview of Terms Used in This Unit:

Evaluation.—That aspect of lesson planning in which a person determines to what extent a learner has achieved a goal.

Response Form.—That aspect of test item design which tells *how* the learner will respond (verbal-with words; descriminator-by choosing among several items; motor skill-by performing a motor skills act.)

Test.—Any activity of any form which proves that a learner has achieved a learning goal. The goal indicator states what the learner must do.

Voluntary response.—A response which a learner makes on his own, without prompting, which indicates his attitude toward a person, place, thing or idea.

Representative response.—A response which one would call "typical" of what one would do to show a change of attitude.

Explain the Universe and Give Two Good Examples!

(Evaluating Learning and Instruction)

● This picture tells the secret of effective evaluation. Study it for a few seconds. Try to decide what it says. Then turn to the next page and answer the question at the top of the page.

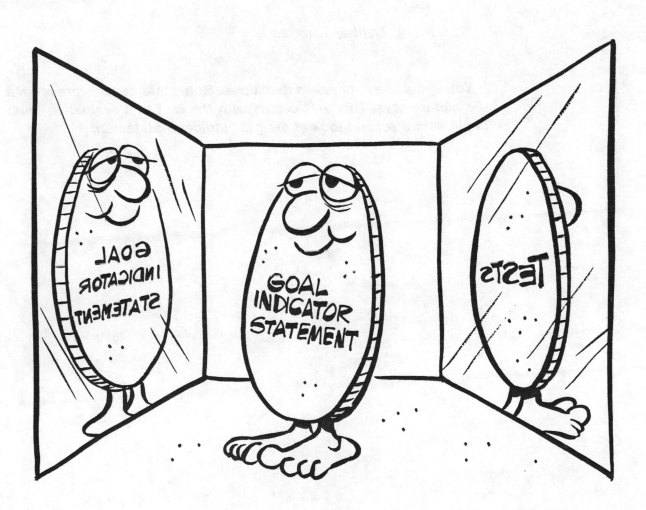

■ Which of the following statements tell(s) what the picture says in regard to evaluation?

_____ 1. The goal-indicator statement and tests form different sides of the same coin.

_____ 2. The goal-indicator and the test (evaluation process) look so much alike that if a teacher has a clearly stated indicator he has clear clues about how to test.

_____ 3. Both 1 and 2.

_____ 4. Neither 1 nor 2.

You should have checked item three. Both statements express what the picture says. This unit begins with the fact that evaluation must begin with a second look at the goal-indicator statement.

● You will remember that unit 2 said that an indicator tells three things: (1) What the learner will do to *prove* he has learned; (2) How well he will perform; and (3) Under what conditions? The indicator tells what the teacher will accept as valid proof that the learner has achieved the goal. The indicator simply describes the test. And the "tests" some teachers use just don't make sense!

Note the similarity between the two statements below. (The indicator statement appears at the left and the test question at the right.)

Indicator	*Test*
The student checks in a list of duties of class officers those which pertain to the class president	In the following list of duties of class officers, identify (check) those which pertain to the class president:

The similarity between indicators (objectives) and tests caused one writer to say, "A prime emphasis on evaluation should be on devising the instructional objectives (indicators). If these goals are specific and operationally stated in terms of observable student behavior, deciding on the measuring instrument will be a relatively easy task." [1]

■ *The teacher who evaluates learning must understand what "test" means. Read the following statements. Which do you think best defines "test"?*

_____ 1. *A written or oral examination which includes one or more questions in such forms as true-false, matching, and essay.*

_____ 2. *Any kind of activity used to prove that the learner has achieved a learning goal.*

Many people would check item one. However, if you check number 1 as correct, how would you "test" one's skill in driving a car? in teaching a Sunday School lesson? The kinds of questions mentioned in number 1 would, of course, test some kinds of learning, but not all. Number 2 calls for "any kind of activity." Test means performance of any kind, used to show that the learner has achieved a learning goal. "Test" includes more than paper and pencil examinations.

---

[1] James W. Popham and Eva L. Baker, *Planning an Instructional Sequence* (Englewood Cliffs, New Jersey, 1970), p. 91.

Some test questions just don't make sense!

■ In the light of the definition of "test," which of the following might serve as tests?

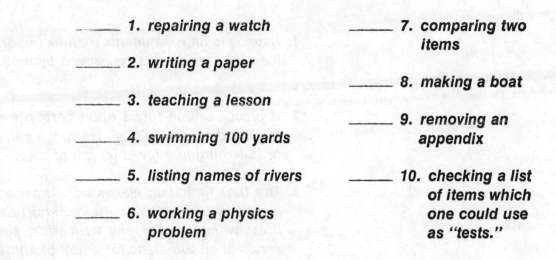

_____ 1. repairing a watch

_____ 2. writing a paper

_____ 3. teaching a lesson

_____ 4. swimming 100 yards

_____ 5. listing names of rivers

_____ 6. working a physics problem

_____ 7. comparing two items

_____ 8. making a boat

_____ 9. removing an appendix

_____ 10. checking a list of items which one could use as "tests."

If you recall that test means "a performance of any kind" you checked all of the items.

■ *Many schools and colleges give written "final exams" of one to four hours in length. Many teachers would call this concept of "final exam" inadequate. Which of the following statements explain(s) why?*

_____ 1. *It tends to cause students to think important only those learnings which can be proved by writing and checking.*

_____ 2. *It places undue focus upon certain kinds of tests. It implies that testing of all learnings can be done orally or in writing in a given length of time.*

_____ 3. *The time limitation allows only those kinds of performances which one can do in a short time. It excludes those which require long term effort, such as writing a series of lesson plans for a unit of study.*

All three explain why the "final exam" concept used by many needs to be broadened. A goal-indicator statement might say that a learner will demonstrate understanding of building design by designing a 100-story building. He scarcely could do it in a two-hour final exam!

This unit will treat first the evaluation of knowledge and understanding. Then focus will shift to evaluation of attitudes. The same principles apply to motor skills. For that reason, this chapter does not deal with motor skills.

Evaluation of Knowledge and Understanding

● Several guidelines should prove helpful as "rules of thumb" in testing or evaluating knowledge and understanding.

1. *Ask for the same or very similar form of response as called for in the goal-indicator statement.*—In Unit 2 you classified indicators (objectives) as "verbal," "discrimination," or "motor." A discrimination indicator calls for the learner to discriminate between items on a test. If the indicators call for a verbal response, the test should as a rule call for an oral or written response. For example, note the verbal form in the following indicator and test item.

(both are verbs)

Indicator:

The learner writes a
100-word paragraph us-
ing a topic sentence
and at least three
points to support the
topic.

Test Item:

Write a 100-word paragraph
using a topic sentence and
at least three points to
support the topic.

Notice that the word *write* calls for a verbal response in both indicator and test.

■ **Do the following indicator and test call for the same form of response?**

Indicator:

The student chooses from three pictures the one which shows the correct hand grip to use in golf.

Test:

Describe the proper grip to use in gripping a golf club.

_____ **Yes**

Why? _____

_____ **No**

The indicator calls for discrimination among three pictures. The test calls for the learner to describe in words the way to hold a gold club. You should have checked "no." The forms do not match.

■ *Study the five indicators and the test items at the right. If the indicators and the test item call for the same form of response, place a check under "appropriate." If not, place a check under "inappropriate."* If inappropriate, explain why?

Indicator	Test Items	Appro-priate	Inappro-priate
1. Given a list of definitions of church select the one which states the Baptist viewpoint.	List five similarities between Catholic and Baptist viewpoints of what "church" means.	_____ Explain:	_____
2. Given a bag of mixed nuts (or students), stack them into piles which contain only one kind of nut.	List ten kinds of nuts (or students).	_____ Explain:	_____
3. Given a written sermon, find the four parts of the sermon as presented in this class.	Write a sermon using the four parts of a sermon as presented in this class.	_____ Explain:	_____
4. Given a list of ten events in history of early Baptists in America, match them with the dates in a second list.	Match these ten events in history of early Baptist in America, with the date on which the event occurred.	_____ Explain:	_____

You should have checked as inappropriate numbers 1, 2, and 3. Only number 4 calls for the same response form. Indicator (objective) number 1 calls for discrimination; the test asks for verbal response (listing). Indicator number 2 calls for discrimination; the test asks for verbal (listing). Indicator 3 calls for discrimination; the test asks for verbal (writing a sermon). Indicator 4 calls for discrimination, as does the test.

● Now, let's look at a second guideline for preparing tests.

2. *Both indicator and test should relate to the same content.*—An indicator and test item may match in the form of response (verbal, discrimination, motor) but fail to deal with the same subject matter.

■ **Look at this example:**
Does the content match?

Indicator	Test
The student lists the names of ten Baptists who fought for religious liberty in America.	**Explain what ten Methodists did to bring about religious liberty.**

_____ Yes

_____ No

You should have checked no. The indicator deals with the subject of names of ten Baptists. The test deals with the subject on what Methodists did. The form (verbal) matches; the content does not.

The third guideline follows.

● 3. *Both indicator and test should reflect the same level of learning.*—You will recall that in knowledge and understanding (cognitive domain) there are six levels of learning: knowledge, comprehension, application, analysis, synthesis, evaluation. For review, study again the following chart which you have seen before:

LEVELS OF LEARNING

(Areas of Knowledge and Understanding)

HIGH		
	EVALUATION	**(Judging value, based on criteria)**
	SYNTHESIS	**(Putting parts together to create something new)**
	ANALYSIS	**(Solving problems systematically; breaking down into parts)**
	APPLICATION	**(Transferring learning to new situations)**
	COMPREHENSION	**(Translating to new forms; interpreting)**
	KNOWLEDGE	**(Memorizing, recalling)**
LOW		

You have learned that a teacher can write an indicator at any level he or she chooses. It follows that the teacher can write test items at any level needed. But the items should reflect the same level as shown in the indicator. If an indicator says a person will *recall* something (knowledge level) the test should ask for recall (knowledge level).

344

■ *Study the following indicator and test item. Then decide whether both reflect the same level of learning.*

Indicator	Test Item
The learner quotes 1 Corinthians 13 from the King James Version of the Bible.	*From the following list of summary statements for 1 Corinthians 13, select the one which states best the central truth.*

Do both indicator and test item reflect the same level of learning?

_____ *Yes*

_____ *No*

The indicator requires the learner to quote word for word 1 Corinthians 13. He does not explain. He quotes. The indicator calls for response at the level of knowledge. The test item requires that the learner study 1 Corinthians in order to find out the central truth. He then selects from two or more summaries the one which states the central truth. The test requires him to perform at the comprehension level. You should have checked no.

■ *In the following exercise, which of the test items would test at the same level of learning called for in the indicator:*

Indicator: *The learner writes a lesson plan on an assigned subject.*

Possible test items: *(Check the appropriate one.)*

_____ 1. *Define in your own words the term "lesson plan," so as to include the three steps in lesson planning.*

_____ 2. *List the steps in the lesson-planning process.*

_____ 3. *Identify in the following plan the steps in the lesson-planning process used in this course.*

_____ 4. *Plan a lesson on "The Rivers of Texas," using the lesson planning process described in the course.*

The indicator calls for response at the synthesis level. It calls for the student to produce a new product—a lesson plan. Test item 1 calls for testing at the comprehension level—lower than the level called for in the indicator. Number 2 calls for response at the knowledge or recall level—the lowest level. Number 3 calls for testing at the analysis level—the learner breaks a plan into its parts. It calls for testing at the level of analysis—a step lower than synthesis. You should have checked number 4. The indicator says "writes a lesson plan." Test item number 4 calls for planning a lesson. They represent the same level.

346

■ *Study the following indicator and test item. Then decide why the test item does not match the indicator.*

Indicator	Test Item
The learner conducts an entire business meeting using Robert's Rules of Order.	The learner handles a "motion to amend" according to Robert's Rules of Order.

Which one of these statements explains why the test item does not match in regard to levels of learning?

_____ 1. *The indicator is written at the evaluation level; the test item at the application level tests at a lower level of learning than specified in the indicator.*

_____ 2. *The indicator specifies performance at the synthesis level while the test item tests at the application level; tests at a lower level of learning than specified in the indicator.*

_____ 3. *The indicator specifies performance at the comprehension level while the test item tests at the memory level; tests at a lower level.*

The indicator calls for response at the synthesis level. The learner synthesizes all he knows about how to conduct a business meeting. The test item reflects the application level. The learner transfers to a new situation the rule for handling motions to amend. The test item does not tell the teacher whether the student can conduct an entire business session. The test does not prove whether the student can "synthesize" the many rules of order to conduct an entire business meeting. You should have checked number 2.

■ **Look now at this list of test items. Match them with the levels of learning shown in the right hand column: (Note: Not all *levels* are represented in the test items.)**

Test Item:

Level of Learning:

_____ 1. Write Carlson's definition of "free church"
and "free state."

1. Knowledge

_____ 2. Assume that you want to
submit to your congress-
man a paper describing
your own concept of
church-state relations.
Write the paper.

2. Comprehension

3. Application

4. Analysis

_____ 3. Assuming Carlson's concept of church-state
relations to be the
biblical concept, de-
cide whether the
following statements
reflect the biblical
concept.

5. Synthesis

6. Evaluation

_____ 4. Write in your own words Carlson's
concept of a free church in a free
state.

_____ 5. On the basis of the following
criteria, determine whether
Carlson's concept of church-
state relations is valid.

_____ 6. Which of the following
drawings pictures Carlson's
concept of church-state
relations?

_____ 7. List the names of three
Baptists who worked for the
concept of "a free church in
a free state."

You may not agree; check your answers with these: one, five, six, two, six, two, one.

348

CHECK YOUR PROGRESS

● This unit has said that test items used in evaluation of knowledge and understanding should (1) call for the same *form* of response called for in the indicator; (2) relate to the same subject with which the indicator deals; and (3) reflect the same level of learning the indicator calls for. [2]

■ *Does the test item for the following indicator reflect use of all three of the guidelines?*

Indicator	Test Item
The pupil translates from English into Spanish a fourth-grade level essay with no more than six errors in grammar.	*Write a paper on the influence of Latin upon modern-day Spanish.*

_____ *Yes*

_____ *No*

You should have checked "no." The test item does not reflect use of all of the guidelines.

---

[2] Teachers interested in delving more deeply into evaluation procedures may refer to such resources as *Classroom Questions: What Kinds?* Holt-Rinehart, Norris Sanders, 1964; and *Effective Questioning, Elementary Level,* Walter R. Borg, Marjorie L. Kelley, and Philip Langer, Macmillan Educational Services, Inc., Beverly Hills, 1970.

■ *There follow several comments on the preceding indicator and test item. Check those which correctly describe the situation.*

_____ 1. *The test item calls for a higher level of learning than the indicator.*

_____ 2. *The test item calls for a lower level of learning than the indicator.*

_____ 3. *The indicator and test item match as to form of response (verbal, discrimination, motor).*

_____ 4. *Both indicator and test item deal with the same subject material.*

_____ 5. *The levels of learning are the same in both indicator and test item.*

You should have checked only one and three. Item one is correct because the test calls for writing a paper (synthesis level) while the indicator calls for translating from English into Spanish (comprehension level). Number 2 is incorrect. The test calls for response at a higher level than the indicator. Number 3 is correct since both call for verbal response. But a test item needs to agree in more than the form of response. Number 4 is not correct—the indicator deals with comprehension of Spanish composition; the test item switches the subject to "the influence of Latin on Spanish." Number 5 is not correct because the indicator and test item reflect different levels of learning.

■ *Now, write the three guidelines for preparing tests of knowledge and understanding.*

1	
2	
3	

To check your answers, refer to the previous pages of this unit.

Evaluation of Attitudes

● As in other kinds of learning, teachers look at goal-indicator statements for clues in evaluating attitude change.

■ *Which of these verses from the Bible suggest attitude evaluation of the basis of indicators of attitude?*

_____ *1. "Ye shall know them by their fruits" (Matt. 7:16).*

_____ *2. "Why call ye me Lord, Lord, and do not the things which I say?" (Luke 6:46).*

We believe that both of these suggest evaluation of attitudes on the basis of typical or representative indicators.

● Previously in this book you have read goal-indicator statements designed for use in teaching for change in attitude. An example follows:

The learner demonstrates an attitude of
concern for the physical needs of refugees
in the United States by doing such things
as:

Interprets for them at employment
agencies;
Visits homes to determine physical needs;
Collects funds for clothing;
Arranges for transportation to doctor's
office;
And so on.

With a little thought, the teacher, along with pupils, could write many other indicators for this goal-indicator statement. The indicators provide clues as to how to evaluate attitudinal learning. As a rule, the teacher finds it hard to prepare test items to evaluate how one feels about something.

● What does the teacher do to measure attitudinal learning? The following guidelines should prove helpful.

1. *Wait for learners to make on their own the responses (or similar ones) called for.*—In teaching for attitude change, the teacher as a rule would not post a list of indicators. The teacher guides learning, then waits with patience for students to make typical responses of their own accord.

■ *Does the following statement tell why the teacher should wait for voluntary responses (sometimes called "approach" responses)?*

If the teacher posted a list of indicators, the pupil could mimic the responses just to please the teacher. The responses might not be genuine.

_____ *Yes*

_____ *No*

We believe it does express the reason why a teacher should withhold from the student the indicators. If a student of his own free will does such things (or like things), the teacher judges that the learner's attitudes have changed.

■ *Which of the following suggest(s) a voluntary response?*

_____ *1. A student turned in as an assignment a scrapbook of articles on the results of drug abuse.*

_____ *2. The student showed the teacher a newspaper clipping he had found on results of drug abuse.*

_____ *3. Both 1 and 2.*

_____ *4. Neither 1 nor 2.*

Number two calls for voluntary response. Students in number one were required to turn in the clippings.

■ *Explain what "voluntary response" means:*

_____

_____

Voluntary response means a response the person makes of his own initiative (or similar words).

● 2. *Accept "representative" responses.*—Teachers could not list all the possible indicators of attitude change. They can only point out representative ones. Goal-indicator statements, which relate to attitudes, need to include a phrase like "by doing such things as . . . " The indicators call for specific responses out of a family of possible ones.

If the teacher waits until the learner does *exactly* what the attitudinal indicators describe, he may wait a lifetime! The teacher learns to judge (evaluate) on the basis of responses similar to those he has called for.

#8 ■ *Explain what "representative responses" means:*

_____

_____

3. *Accept the fact that one cannot measure attitudinal learning with the same ease with which he measures knowledge, understanding, and motor skills learning.*—Teachers find it difficult to say "how well" one should do when it comes to attitude change. They have few standards by which to judge *how well* a person has done in changing attitude. The teacher should ask himself, Which level of attitude change does the learner seem to have achieved?

For example:

Does the learner's life-style reflect the attitude?   (Characterization level)

Has the learner at least stopped to pay attention?   (Responding level)

Has the learner made a commitment to an idea, person, et cetera?   (Valuing level)

Does the learner ponder how one value relates to another in making decisions?   (Organization level)

CHECK YOUR PROGRESS

● Now, write the three guidelines for evaluating attitudinal change.

1	
2	
3	

Check your answers with the guidelines presented in this section.

**PUTTING
IT
ALL
TOGETHER
(THE LESSON PLAN)**

UNIT 13

The Aha! Moment—Putting It All Together

● You have studied the three essential concepts in planning for learning. You have learned to write learning goals. You have learned to create learning activities related to the goals. You have learned to test whether the learner has learned.

Now we put these three parts together and give them a name: *lesson plan*. This unit should help you "put it all together" into a teaching tool—a lesson plan.

What guidelines can help the teacher put the parts together into a plan?

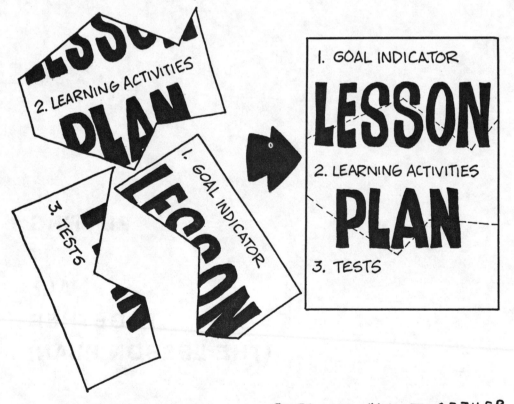

THIS CHAPTER . . . . PUTS IT ALL TOGETHER

You will need approximately 1 hour to complete this unit.

In finding the answers, look first at a sample lesson plan which includes the three parts—goal-indicator, learning activities, and test. The very simple lesson plan which follows deals with the subject, "The Writers of the Books of the New Testament." The goal-indicator, learning activities, and the tests all relate to that subject. Read the entire plan before going further. Then refer back to the plan to answer the questions which follow the lesson plan.

Lesson Plan Number One

Topic: "Names of Writers of New Testament Books"		
GOAL-INDICATOR	LEARNING ACTIVITIES FROM WHICH TO CHOOSE	TEST
Goal The learner demonstrates knowledge of the names of the writers of the books of the New Testament. *Indicator* . . . by matching a list of New Testament books with a list of authors.	1. At the beginning of the lesson, show the pupils a chart of books of the New Testament and their authors. Ask a pupil to read them aloud. 2. Disbribute flashcards to groups of two class members each. Ask each of the members to drill the other member, showing first the name of the book, and confirming answers by flashing the other side of the card. 3. Conduct an "author-naming bee" similar to a spelling bee, using two teams of pupils. 4. Give each pupil a list of authors of books of the Bible, including Old Testament authors. Ask pupils to classify them according to whether they are New Testament authors. 5. Conduct an "author-naming game." Call out the name of one New Testament book. Ask one student to tell the author. Then ask that student to call out the name of another book and to call on any other pupil to name the author.	Match the following list of books of the New Testament with the list of writers provided.

■ *In the exercises which follow, you will need to refer back to the preceding lesson plan.*

Study the goal-indicator statement for the lesson plan. Which of the following learning outcomes did the leader use?

_____ 1. Motor skill

_____ 2. Understanding

_____ 3. Knowledge

_____ 4. Attitude

The teacher had selected knowledge as the primary learning outcome (kind of learning). Notice that it deals with remembering facts. You should have checked number three, knowledge.

■ *Refer again to the preceding lesson plan number one. Since the leader chose knowledge as the kind of learning needed, which of these sets of guidelines for teaching would he use to work out the learning activities?*

Set 1 The guidelines related to:	Set 2 The guidelines related to:	Set 3 The guidelines related to:	Set 4 The guidelines related to:
translation discovering relationships defining concepts using in practical ways breaking material down into parts problem solving . . . and so on	*active responding use of more than one of the senses advance organizers knowledge of results numerous and varied activities . . . and so on*	*step-by-step demonstration guidance on first attempts verbalization repeated practice . . . and so on*	*personal example reading or hearing about persons positive action authoritative sources sharing in groups reflecting on experiences . . . and so on*

You will remember that Unit 6 dealt with guidelines to use when teaching for knowledge. It included the guidelines outlined in set number 2. This means the teacher-leader could use that list of guidelines or principles to help determine the right activities to use to help learners remember the books of the New Testament and their authors.

363

■ *Now, to help make clear how the teacher-leader used the learning guidelines to decide on learning activities in lesson plan one, do the following exercise. The left-hand column lists again some of the main activities shown in the short lesson plan presented earlier. Match the activity with the guideline each activity seems to use most. (Only two guidelines are listed. Choose between them.)*

Activity	Guideline
_____ *At the beginning of the lesson show the pupils a chart of books of the New Testament and their authors.*	*1. Provide for immediate knowledge of results.*
_____ *Distribute flashcards. Ask each member to drill another member on names and authors by flashing a bookname card. After the other person answers, let him see the other side for the answer.*	*2. Provide activities which use advance organizers.*
_____ *Conduct an "author-naming-bee" similar to a spelling bee, using two teams of pupils. When a person misses the name of an author after being given the name of the book, he goes to the foot of the line.*	

You probably answered in this way: 2, 1, 1. In the first activity, the pupils saw in advance the total list of names. In both the second and third activities the pupils received knowledge of results. The flashcards provided knowledge of results when the pupil turned the card over. In the last one, pupils had to know results of their answer in order to determine their place in line. The teacher-leader deliberately used the two guidelines by using the three activities.

■ *Now look at the indicator and the test in lesson plan one. The word which tells what the pupil will do to prove he has learned appears in both. What is it?* _____

The word match *appears in both.*

#9

■ *In lesson plan one the teacher-leader deliberately used the guidelines or principles of learning in order to think of the right kinds of activities. We may picture this process in another way. Study the following diagram which some call the "scissortailed arrow." Then in the blanks below the diagram, write a summary statement which explains what it says.*

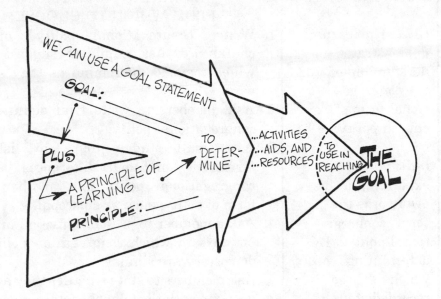

Now, summarize what the illustration says about lesson planning.

_____

_____

If you "followed the arrows," you said something like this: We can use a goal statement plus a guideline or principle of learning to help us determine the right kinds of activities, aids, and resources to use in reaching the goal. To explain further, a goal tells us whether to teach for knowledge, understanding, skill, or attitude. When we know that, we can know which guidelines or principles of learning to use to help us think of activities. When the pupil engages in the activities, hopefully he achieves the goal.

This oversimplified lesson plan shows how the teacher-leader can put the goal-indicator statement, learning activities, and test together to form a lesson plan. One can follow the same process with more difficult lessons.

● Now let's look at a less simple lesson plan (lesson plan two). The subject of this one is "The Congregational Form of Church Government." Study it before answering the questions which follow it.

Lesson Plan Number Two

Lesson Topic: "The Congregational Form of Church Polity"		
GOAL-INDICATOR	LEARNING ACTIVITIES FROM WHICH TO CHOOSE	TEST
Goal: The learner demonstrates understanding of the congregational form of church polity. *Indicators:* By explaining in his own words the term "congregational polity." By determining which of three recorded church business sessions reflect use of congregational polity.	1. Write "congregational polity" on the chalkboard. Ask pupils to suggest words which come to their mind as they see the word. 2. Ask members to write trial definitions of congregational polity. 3. Ask small study groups to list four similarities and four differences between congregational polity and another given form of polity, such as episcopal. 4. Ask a member to present a five-minute talk on ways in which congregation polity and democracy are similar. 5. Ask members to state whether they agree or disagree with the following statement and to give reasons: "Congregational polity is an example of pure democracy at work." 6. Ask members to draw pictures representing congregational polity or government. Then ask them to explain to one another their drawings. 7. Ask members to outline the book, *Forms of Church Polity.* 8. Ask members to listen to tape recordings of excerpts from business meetings to determine which forms of polity they represent.	1. Explain in your own words the term, *congregational polity.* 2. Listen to the following three recorded church business sessions. Identify which reflects congregational polity.

In the exercises which follow, you will need to refer back to the lesson plan above.

■ *Study the goal-indicator for lesson plan two. Which of the following learning outcomes did the leader use?*

_____ 1. *Knowledge*

_____ 2. *Understanding*

_____ 3. *Motor skill*

_____ 4. *Attitude*

The teacher had selected understanding as the primary learning outcome. The leader evidently wanted the learner to do more than learn facts for recall. You should have checked number two.

■ *Since the leader chose understanding as the primary learning out-come, which of the following sets of guidelines would he use to work out the learning activities for lesson plan two?*

Set 1 The guidelines related to:	Set 2 The guidelines related to:	Set 3 The guidelines related to:	Set 4 The guidelines related to:
translation *discovering re-lationships* *defining con-cepts* *using in practi-cal ways* *breaking mate-rial down into parts* *problem solving* *. . . and so on*	*active respond-ing* *use of more than one of the senses* *advance or-ganizers* *knowledge of results* *numerous and varied ac-tivities* *. . . and so on*	*step-by-step demonstration* *guidance on first attempts* *verbalization* *repeated prac-tice* *. . . and so on*	*personal exam-ple* *reading or hear-ing about persons* *positive action* *authoritative sources* *sharing in groups* *reflecting on experiences* *. . . and so on*

Hopefully you recognized one as the list of guidelines especially related to developing understanding. This means that the teacher used this set of guidelines as guides in deciding on learning activities. The teacher considered each guideline or principle and asked, How can I deliberately use this principle to develop learning activities which will help pupils understand forms of church government pol-ity? [1]

---

[1] At this point one should remember that the guidelines listed for the different kinds of learning seem to be especially appropriate for that kind of learning. *However,* they apply to some extent to all the other kinds of learning. In Unit 1 we called this occurrence "diffusion of learning." That means that when we teach for understanding something happens also to attitudes, knowledge, and skills. Teachers and leaders simply focus on given guidelines for achieving a specific kind of learning.

■ *Now, to help us understand how the teacher-leader used the guidelines to develop the learning activities in the lesson plan, match each of the following three activities from the lesson plan with the guideline it puts to work. (The activities come from lesson plan two shown above.) You may need to refer back to Unit 7 for a review of the guidelines related to teaching for understanding. We have listed only three of the guidelines in this exercise.*

Activities	Guidelines
_____ Outline the book, Forms of Church Polity	1. Use activities in which the learner discovers relationships among ideas and concepts
_____ Write "congregational" on the chalkboard. Ask pupils to suggest synonyms for the term.	2. Involve the learners in activities in which they break material down into its parts.
_____ Ask members to draw a picture which represents "congregational government." Then ask them to explain their drawings.	3. Provide activities in which the learner translates ideas into new forms.

We would choose these answers: 2, 1, and 3. Remember that when a person outlines something given to him—something already written—he must analyze the content and break it down into its parts. Therefore, outlining the book Forms of Church Polity calls for use of the guideline or principle of "breaking down into parts."

When pupils suggest words associated with "congregational" they use the guideline "discover relationships."

When they draw a picture representing congregational polity, they "translate" words into pictures. Then from their own drawing they translate back into words. They use the guideline or principle of translation.

So, in this lesson plan, the teacher-trainer deliberately applied the guidelines to aid in thinking of the right kinds of activities.

369

■ *Now look at the two indicators and the test for lesson plan two on "The Congregational Form of Church Polity." Which two statements tell what the learner will do to indicate achievement of the goal?*

1. _____
2. _____

The learner does two things: (1) explains in his own words; and (2) determines which of the three recordings represent congregational polity.

Again, the teacher-leader worked out a goal-indicator statement, used the guidelines to help determine activities, then tested using the process described in the goal-indicator.

Now, study this additional lesson plan number three. It's form differs from the other two. Simply note how the learning activities relate to the kind of learning expressed in the goal. Note also how the test corresponds to the activity described in the goal-indicator statement.

Lesson Plan Number Three	
1. The goal-indicator statement:	The learner demonstrates understanding of the meaning of Christian love by paraphrasing 1 Corinthians 13.
2. Appropriate learning activities:	1. Ask members to suggest synonyms for the word *love*. 2. Ask members to compare similarities and differences in three different translations of 1 Corinthians 13. 3. Ask members to report on dictionary definitions of key words in 1 Corinthians 13—such as faith, hope, insist, and so on. 4. As preparation for the class session, ask members to read silently the chapter at least fifteen times, making notes of insights gained each time. Call for reports. 5. And so on . . .
3. Test item:	Provide each person with a copy of the King James Version of 1 Corinthians 13. Ask them to paraphrase the chapter, keeping the same meaning.

● For another visual review of the planning process presented in this book, read carefully this chart.

LEARNING GOAL	ACTIVITIES	TEST

The goal tells us which kind of learning:
    knowledge
    understanding
    skill
    attitude
	The kind of learning desired gives us clues as to which guidelines or principles of learning to focus on. We use the guidelines to help us think of the right kinds of learning activities. Then learners use the activities to help reach the goal.	After using the activities, we test to find out whether the person has learned. We base the test on the indicators.

Now, you're on your own. Now practice writing a lesson plan of your own. Use a subject like the following, or choose a Sunday School lesson of your own.

The Ten Commandments

The Parable of the Good Samaritan

What Redemption Means

Good luck!

**SPECIAL HELP
FOR
SPECIAL PEOPLE**

UNIT 14

Master the Techniques of Directive Writing
(For editors and writers of lesson plans)

The editor decides! He decides whether the nineteen guidelines for directive writing in this unit have merit. Those who do directive writing follow the editor's guidance. But many editors do find the guidelines in this unit helpful.

Most teachers and trainers have to write lesson plans. They can do a better job if they master a few techniques of directive writing. The guidelines in this unit should help lesson planners express clearly what they want to say.

Like a good recipe, directive writing instructs clearly and concisely. The reader follows the instructions to achieve a goal.

1. *Use the command form of descriptive verbs.*—The use of the command form of verbs results in tight writing. Excess words fall by the wayside. A descriptive verb leaves no doubt in the mind of the reader as to what he should do.

The use of "may" and "might" and "perhaps" weakens a recipe. The chef himself decides whether he will do what the recipe says. The command form of verbs which describe action needs less explanation. Few writers can travel along with their "recipes" to explain the vague points.

Descriptive verbs pinpoint action. Other verbs leave the reader in doubt as to what he should do. Sheet lightning verbs like "use" and "have" and "give" don't hit anything. Readers need to see a visual image of the action.

You will need approximately 20 minutes to complete this unit.

■ *Which of these verbs in command form describe a precise action?*

_____ 1. List *the reasons.*

_____ 2. Present *the problem.*

_____ 3. Use *the chalkboard.*

_____ 4. Paint *it red.*

_____ 5. Read *it aloud.*

You probably checked one, four, and five. The verbs "present" and "use" call for answers to the question, How? And that brings up the next guideline.

375

● 2. *Make the question "how?" a part of your writing personality.*—Tell the reader *how* to do. The command, "Use the chalkboard to explain how verbs differ from adverbs" does not tell the reader *how* to use the chalkboard.

■ **Circle in this activity the verbs which describe clearly what the leader should do.**

Draw a line down the middle of the chalkboard. Caption one side "verbs"; the other, "adverbs." Ask pupils to suggest in rapid-fire order some examples of each. Ask a pupil to write the examples in the appropriate column.

The verbs draw, caption, ask, and write describe actions.

● 3. *Make that 180° about-face—spotlight pupil activity.*—Focus on the pupil learning, not on the teacher teaching. Of course, sometimes the teacher or leader must do something! And at times, leader and pupils work together. Apply this test to your writing: Does the activity call for learner response? "Explain the meaning of democracy" calls for the learner to act.

Focus on ways to lead the pupil to discover things for himself. But remember that the leader has a role, too. Just keep a good balance between leader activity and learner activity.

■ *Which of the following focus on pupil action rather than teacher action?*

_____ 1. Ask each pupil to write a trial definition of "peace."

_____ 2. Draw on the chalkboard the following chart.

_____ 3. Ask a pupil to draw on the chalkboard the following chart.

_____ 4. Point out on the map the location of Judah and Egypt.

_____ 5. Distribute to each pupil an outline map. Ask him to write the names Judah and Egypt in the correct places.

You probably indicated numbers one, three and five.

■ *Change each of the following statements so as to call for the pupil to act.*

1. *Give a brief lecture on the causes of the Civil War.* _____

_____

2. *Prepare a montage of pictures showing the results of air pollution.* _____

_____

_____

Perhaps you rewrote the activities like this: (1) Lecture briefly on the "Causes of the American Civil War." Ask group 1 to listen *for* the causes from the viewpoint of the South; group 2 to listen for causes from the viewpoint of the North. Call for reports. (2) Ask the pupils to cut from magazines and newspapers pictures showing the results of air pollution. Ask groups of three to combine their pictures and make a montage. Call on a member of each group to explain the group's work.

The second rewrite calls for more pupil action than the first. Number 1 injects pupil response into an otherwise passive method. Even when a leader lectures he can arrange for learner response.

4. *Suggest feasible activities which learners can perform.*—Ask, Could the teacher or pupils do this if they wanted to?

■ **Which of these activities suggest(s) action which most learners could do?**

_____ 1. Draw on poster board 22 by 28 inches a portrait of Abraham Lincoln. Display it before the group.

_____ 2. Ask a pupil to bring and show to the group a portrait of Abraham Lincoln.

_____ 3. Ask each pupil to take from his pocket a Lincoln head penny.

Most pupils could locate a Lincoln head penny, as number 3 suggests. The simpler the activity, the greater the chance the trainer will use it. Before asking a person to do something, count the obstacles the teacher-trainer must hurdle in order to use it. How many leaders would actually draw a portrait of Lincoln?

■ List several "hurdles" a teacher-trainer would have to overcome in order to display a handmade portrait of Abraham Lincoln, 22 by 28 inches.

1. _____

2. _____

3. _____

4., 5., 6. . . . _____

You may have included: Find some newsprint. Get money to pay for the poster board. Decide which color. Find a portrait to copy. Sketch the drawing. Hunt for an eraser. Cover up the smudges. Look for file 13. Recover it from file 13. Find a table on which to display it. Pull your hair out! And so on. These absurd actions overdo the matter. But as a rule, the more feasible the activity the greater the chance the teacher-trainer will use it.

Follow the advice of the sunk-in-the-mire student who said to use the KISS formula! *K*eep *I*t *S*imple, *s*tupid! Some lesson plans include complex, hard-to-follow ideas. Use the simplest learning aid or activity which will do the job well. If a simple handout given to the learners will do the job as well as a costly film, choose the simpler of the two.

● 5. *Make it say the same thing to everybody.*—The same words sometimes mean different things to different people. Sometimes words do not mean anything to any people. "A yellowish fruit that grows on trees" may suggest to a Canadian a golden delicious apple; to a Central American, a papaya. It depends upon the person's likes and background.

■ *What does the following directive mean? Rewrite it to make it clear in meaning.*

On the chalkboard draw two six-inch squares. Color one red; the other green.

_____

_____

_____

You probably wrote something like this: On the chalkboard draw two six-inch squares. Color one red; the other green.

6. *Provide a way of escape—one or more other ways to do it.*—No two pupils learn in the same way. No two teacher-trainers use with equal results the same activities. Provide other choices. For example, "Display a portrait of Abraham Lincoln, or ask each member to take from his pocket a Lincoln head penny." Suggest items which the teacher-trainer or the pupils will likely have at hand.

■ **Rewrite the statements below so as to suggest an alternative.**

1. Ask a policeman to speak for ten minutes on "Causes of Crime." _____

2. Ask a pupil to write on butcher paper the list of topics for the unit. _____

3. Display a live mink in a cage. _____

4. Divide the group into twenty groups of six persons each. _____

You probably wrote things like this: "Ask a pupil to interview a policeman and make a report." "Ask a pupil to write on newsprint or the want ad section of a newspaper the list of topics." "Display a picture of a mink in a cage." (If one can find such a picture!) At least, let the leader substitute a rabbit for the mink! "Divide the group into small study groups." (What if the teacher only has six persons in his class?)

7. *Integrate the "systems" within the plan.*—Systems suggest the parts of a plan. They include resources and activities of many kinds which the teacher-trainer and pupils will use to achieve a goal. In man's flights to the moon, many "systems" worked in proper harmony to achieve the end result. All systems reside in a lesson plan. Systems in a lesson plan include reference books, learning aids, textbooks (if needed), the leader and pupils themselves, the *Leader's Guide,* learning goals, tests, and so on.

To "integrate the systems" means to ensure that each part does what it should do. The secret: make sure that the use of each "system" helps learners achieve the goal.

8. *Do away with irrelevant stuff.*—"Content" [1] in the usual sense of the word, belongs in a resource book or article, not in the lesson plan. At times, when the added "content" requires only one or two lines, one may include it in the plan.

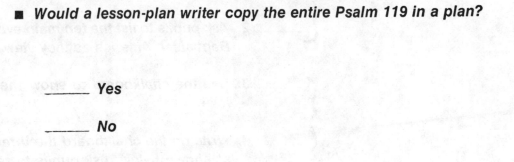

■ *Would a lesson-plan writer copy the entire Psalm 119 in a plan?*

_____ Yes

_____ No

The longest psalm would have no place in a lesson plan. Writers would refer the reader to the Bible.

---

[1] "Content" technically means both ideas and activities. We use it here to mean only ideas or subject matter.

9. *Avoid "cliff-hangers."*—Some writers find it hard to think in terms of the specifics. How? and Why? They end up with cliff-hanger plans. They tell the teacher-trainer to do something, but the something does not suggest how to go about it. For example: Display a chart of the steps in the planning process. So what? The lesson planner needs to complete the activity. Does showing a chart have educational value in and of itself? It may have some, but it can have more. Suggest how to involve the pupil actively in regard to the chart. Ask, What will he do with it? Teacher-trainers have more resources than this world dreams of. But many do not know how to turn a cliff-hanger into an activity which calls for response.

■ *In the list below, check the "cliff-hanger" in each pair of activities.*

_____ **1. Present the filmstrip.**

_____ **2. Ask pupils to list the ten main events in the history of Baptists in America as they view the filmstrip.**

_____ **3. Use the chalkboard to show the three meanings of love.**

_____ **4. Write on the chalkboard the three meanings of love, as shown below. Ask pupils to select the one which means agape.**

You should have checked numbers 1 and 3 as "cliff-hangers." Neither tells what to do nor how to do it!

10. *Use active verbs.*—With practice a writer can avoid the overuse of forms of "to be." These include "been," "have been," "was," "to be," and especially "is" and "are."

■ **Review this chapter. Write in this blank the number of times you see a form of "to be."** _____

We think you found none. Right?—except those included in this section (Section 10). It was not our intention that there be any. If there were, then the article ought to be changed!

Active verbs describe action. The reader can see the precise action involved.

11. *Avoid the "stick-up."*—Suggest resources which the reader can afford. Cost may cause the reader to decide not to use a resource. If the leader can borrow an expensive resource, well and good. If he cannot, don't count on his using it.

■ **Would you expect a large number of leaders to acquire the resource which this activity suggests?**

Display the latest model Rolls Royce sedan.

_____ **Yes**

_____ **No**

● 12. *Explain where to find it.*—Instead of "Give to each pupil a copy of the pamphlet, *Managing Your Money*," say, "Give to each member a copy of the pamphlet *Managing Your Money*. (Order from the Christian Life Commission, Southern Baptist Convention, 460 James Robertson Parkway, Nashville, Tennessee, 37219. x cents per copy.)" Of course the address requires space. But does the goal require use of the pamphlet or not? Some writers prefer to place the address in a bibliography. In that case, the lesson plan says, "(See bibliography, page 9.)"

● 13. *Inform the producer that you want to suggest his resource.*—Help him avoid the panic of the empty cupboard! Teaching plans in lesson course periodicals do get responses! One line in a teaching-training plan in a periodical can result in thousands of orders. The supplier may not have the items in stock. In this case the suggestion loses its value. Tell the supplier when you plan to suggest an item. Inform him how many orders he may expect. One might even ask him for permission to suggest the resource! Teachers and trainers develop bad attitudes toward lesson plans when they receive a "sorry, out of stock" answer.

14. *Follow a valid plan for planning.*—Most plans for planning include at least three parts: (1) a goal statement; (2) a set of learning activities which relate to the goal, and (3) test items of some kind.

Think in terms of the entire unit. Some guides for single sessions include all three parts. All guides ought to include goals and learning activities. Sometimes a test will appear only once or twice in a unit. At times, a teacher-trainer may decide to include tests only with the last session. He risks certain dangers, however, when he delays test activities.

What the writer knows about the target group helps him decide the degree to which he will follow a planning scheme. A target group which needs a lot of guidance needs lesson plans which follow a logical sequence pattern. The suggestions "flow" and "make sense" to the reader as he reads through the plan.

Those who need less help may prefer a list of possible activities from which to choose. Then they develop their own sequence of activities. Such plans sometimes use an introduction like this: "From the list of activities which follows, select the most helpful ones. Include them in your own lesson plan."

15. *Avoid the methods rut.*—The best of lesson plan writers tend to suggest certain methods and aids too often. One who writes a series of guides for a unit of study will likely fall into a methods rut. He may not recognize it. But the planner may have used too often a good method or aid—small study groups, lecture, panel, brainstorming, flipcharts. To avoid this trap, use a control sheet like this one:

LESSON NUMBER

METHODS AND AIDS	1	2	3	4	5	6	7	8	9	10
PANEL	✓		✓				✓		✓	✓
LECTURE		✓		✓	✓					
SMALL STUDY GROUPS	✓	✓	✓		✓	✓	✓		✓	✓
CASE STUDY		✓			✓		✓			
FLIPCHART	✓	✓	✓	✓	✓	✓		✓	✓	✓
CHALKBOARD	✓		✓				✓			✓

■ **List from the chart above, the methods or aids which the planner used too often.**

1. _____

2. _____

The planner seemed to feel that small study groups would do all things for all lessons. He had a lot of enthusiasm for flipcharts, too!

Now, let's soften this guideline a bit. The lesson planner should use the *best* method for the purpose, even if it means using it often. The learning goal and target group *could* dictate the use of a given approach in every session.

● 16. *Suggest the right enrichment materials.*—A teacher's guide provides a way for the lesson planner to expand the scope of the basic resource. (With permission of the editor, of course.) The lesson plan serves as the "heart" of the instructional system.

Suggest resources other than the basic one if the resources would enrich the learning. Many plans have their basis in a textbook or some other resource. Some pupils want to delve more deeply into the study. Suggest resources "for further study."

● 17. *Provide for ability levels in the target group.*—Most large target groups consist of subgroups which differ widely in background and ability. In this case, two or more plans, each geared to a given level in a target group, provide better results. The creative teacher-trainer will choose from all plans to build one of his own. Some writers include one plan which uses a simple, more traditional approach. Another may require the user to do more of the planning himself. It may use more complex methods and aids. Some groups require a step-by-step plan; others prefer to build their own plan, using "germ ideas" as a basis.

● 18. *Apply the "would-I-do-it-myself?" test.*—Some writers would not or could not use their own plans! Ask yourself, Can the reader translate this into action? Some complex plans defy use. Some plans suggest children's work for mature learners.

And now for the last guideline.

● 19. *Soften all the commands and the imperatives with the milk of human kindness and courtesy.*—Talk to the teacher or trainer in tones which convey your respect for him. Use the command form, but know that the reader has integrity, too.

These and other guidelines should take you a long way toward becoming a good writer of lesson plans.